Designing the City

Designing the City

Towards a more sustainable urban form

Hildebrand Frey

SPON PRESS
Taylor & Francis Group

London and New York

First published 1999
by E & FN Spon

Reprinted 2001
by Spon Press
11 New Fetter Lane, London EC4P 4EE

Simultaneously published in the USA and Canada
by Routledge
29 West 35th Street, New York, NY 10001

Spon Press is an imprint of the Taylor & Francis Group

Typeset in Optima 9/11pt by
J&L Composition Ltd, Filey, North Yorkshire
Printed and bound in Great Britain by
Bell & Bain Ltd, Glasgow

British Library Cataloguing in Publication Data
A catalogue record for this book is available from the British Library

ISBN 0 419 22110 7

Library of Congress Cataloging in Publication Data
Frey, Hildebrand, 1940–
     Designing the city: towards a more sustainable form/Hildebrand
Frey.
        p.   cm.
     Includes bibliographical references and index.
     ISBN 0–419–22110–7
     1. City planning—Economic aspects.   2. City planning—
Environmental aspects.   3. Urban policy.   4. Urban ecology.
5. City and town life.   6. City planning—Scotland—Glasgow.
7. Glasgow (Scotland)—Social conditions.   8. Glasgow (Scotland)—
Environmental conditions.   I. Title.
HT165.5.F74 1999   98–31105
307.1′216—dc21   CIP

Contents

Acknowledgements

This book would not have come about in its present form without the help of a number of people and institutions to whom I owe my thanks.

There are first and foremost my mentors – Professor Peter Reed and Professor Frank Walker from the Department of Architecture and Building Science at the University of Strathclyde and Professor John Punter at the Department of City and Regional Planning at the University of Wales – who have tried, successfully or unsuccessfully, to keep my sentences short and my arguments, with which they may or may not agree, in the right structure. Their critical and constructive comments were of considerable value.

Then there are those who have helped me to generate the illustrations. With the assistance of Adrian Stewart, Scott Neilly started by generating the base map and soon found the task somewhat complex and difficult. I am particularly indebted to Robin McClory who had enough patience to cope with huge computer files and minute details of the maps (many of which are lost in this publication but may be useful in others), and who had to endure the oddities and annoying idiosyncrasies of computer hardware and software.

All maps of the city region and conurbation of Glasgow (Chapter 5) and of the districts of Glasgow (Chapter 6) are based upon Ordnance Survey 1:25,000 Pathfinder maps and are reproduced with the Permission of the Controller of Her Majesty's Stationery Office, © Crown Copyright. Licence no. 273880/1. My thanks go to Ordnance Survey because without this licence the illustration of the design interventions at regional, conurbation and district level would have been impossible.

The Planning Department of Glasgow City Council kindly gave permission to trace map information from the 1995 *Ward Profiles* and the 1997/98 *Factsheets* which made it possible to illustrate the growth of the city, the location of CDAs and peripheral estates and the population distribution *(Figs 4.01b, 4.08, 4.15, 4.32 and 4.36)*. Though the statistics used in this book are not entirely up to date the general conditions are believed not to have altered to a degree that would invalidate the findings. Essex County Council kindly gave permission to retrace Fig. 4.51 of *A Design Guide for Residential Areas*, December 1973 *(Fig. 4.30)*.

Thanks also to Scottish Enterprise for permission to reproduce four of their aerial photographs *(Figs 4.20, 4.27a, 4.31 and 4.38)*. These photographs are the property of Scottish Enterprise, who possess copyright, and may not be reproduced in any fashion without the Agency's express prior consent in writing.

Last but not least, thanks go to the Department of Architecture and Building Science of the University of Strathclyde, who granted me leave of absence and relieved me of some administrative tasks. Without this additional time having been made available to me, the book would not have been finished in time.

Introduction

Books about urban design and about the city appear in ever-increasing numbers and many of them talk about sustainable urban development and living. They frequently start with a discussion of the destructive impact of our way of (mostly urban) life on the regional and global environment and come up with a series of programmes of behavioural changes, specifically the change from car dependency to public transport and the change from a linear to a cyclic metabolism, i.e. from dumping waste to recycling. Yet, important as all these issues are, few publications attempt an analysis in depth of the role which the physical form and structure of today's city plays in this process of environmental destruction, and few proposals are made as to how the city should be physically changed to improve its environmental impact. In fact, as this book will show later, much of the current discussion of a sustainable city form and structure is confused and inconclusive.

This book is about the city's and the city region's physical form and structure. It investigates physical changes that may make the city work better, be more people-friendly and less harmful to the local and global environment. The book grew out of a study of cities in Europe and the USA and the way in which they attempt to control urban development and improve the urban environment. Many set up urban development frameworks for the city at large, within its region, that not only contain land-use plans and cover socio-economic issues but also address the city's physical form and structure.

Key Arguments Against and For Strategic Planning and Urban Design

Urban development frameworks that include plans for the physical aspects of the city and city region are not readily available in the UK, and there are many who actually regard them as suspect in one way or another if not downright counter-productive. Many arguments are brought forward against strategic planning and designing and some of them are rehearsed here in an attempt to expose their implausibility.

Designing the city and city region? Today the city is more than ever shaped by economic forces.

Today's city, so the argument goes, is shaped more than ever by our way of life, by the communications and transport technology we use, and by market forces. Venturi *et al.* (1972) recognised these factors as being responsible for the specific urban and architectural characteristics of Las Vegas – competition in a local, regional and global market on the one hand and the motorcar as prime means of transport on the other. Tokyo is a striking example of the way in which the city changes as a result of global economic forces, with many of its buildings having an average life span of a mere three years. Such a city is no longer the result of, or even influenced by, formal, spatial and structural ideals. Urban planning and urban design have little if any influence on this process of urban development and change. As Venturi *et al.* put it, the pattern of the city is the result of the technology of movement and communication and the economic value of land. Today's city form and structure are as undetermined as today's urban society, for which individual needs seem to be more important than collective values. An attempt to control development might actually deter inward investment and would therefore be counter-productive.

Such arguments may be understandable in a situation in which urban planning, and even more so urban design, play only a weak and much reduced role in urban development control. The acceptance of an enterprise culture seems to include the acceptance of handing over development control to the forces which drive this culture. Consequently, the city is the expression of the needs and wants of international and economically powerful forces using the city as their playing field. Such a city is not planned and designed for people according to traditional principles, based on collective values; in any case, we are advised that 'there is no such thing as society' and so everybody is on his or her own. Such a city just happens.

But there are many cities in Europe, the USA and elsewhere – Birmingham, Berlin, Antwerp, Barcelona, Portland (Oregon), to name but a few examples – in which urban planning and notably also urban design make an essential contribution in development guidance. For these cities, playing a role in a global market does not seem to imply the inevitability of surrendering urban development control to global economic forces. Maybe these cities have understood the lesson of 'a century of industrialisation during which market forces, left to their own devices, fail utterly to produce a humane environment' (Professor Colin Buchanan, in Tibbalds, 1992, p. 5). Maybe they have also understood that a city that surrenders development control to economic forces does not necessarily benefit from consequent gains in the global market. The question arises as to why many of our cities seem not to have learned the same lessons or why many seem unaware of and irritated by the chaotic, anti-urban and hostile environment generated as a result of self-centred development in many parts of our cities.

Designing the city and city region? With a few exceptions, towns and cities have in the past developed incrementally and without a masterplan with very good results. When in the 1950s and 1960s grand-scale master plans were developed things went dramatically wrong. Such an approach should never be repeated.

It is indisputable that, with the exception of a few cases of 'ideal cities', urban development is incremental, the result of a sequence of independent, frequently speculative interventions and development projects that are gradually woven together to form a town, city, metropolis, none of which will ever have a finite form or structure. Cities will continue to change, grow or shrink, expand or contract, in order to adapt to changing socioeconomic conditions. So it is understandable that the question is raised of why the city should be planned and designed as an entity if its form and structure emerge and change in a long and ongoing development process and are never finite unless the city is to become a museum. Even a city like Glasgow – which later will play a role in investigations of urban forms and structures – with its gridiron pattern that seems to show strong evidence of spatial planning, was not designed as an entity, as a whole. The city plan emerged as a result of the process of the implementation of many speculative development projects, a process which Alexander *et al.* (1987) see as being responsible for the 'wholeness' of traditional towns. In contrast, the master plan approach adopted in the 1950s and 1960s resulted in the loss of much of the historical fabric and traditional

development pattern, and the 'brave new world' soon proved in many ways inadequate.

Regarding incremental process and speculative development, the situation is not much different today, only the economic forces at work now are no longer local but international, global, and they are not out to create that 'wholeness'; they are only interested in their individual unrelated acts. Historic incremental speculative development was based on a commonly accepted set of development rules and patterns and generated a strongly ordered urban environment; current incremental speculative development adopts a free-for-all approach and generates 'opportunistic chaos' (Tibbalds, 1992, p. 5). Admittedly, many of the functionalist changes in the city have failed because they were based on a misconceived concept of the city and on inadequate technology; but to have no plan at all obviously does not generate an acceptable city form and structure either.

Designing the city or city region? The city form is never finite, always changing. Design tends to freeze form and structure and to prevent the city from adapting to changing socio-economic conditions.

There are many examples of the impact of a strong formalistic and rigid design concept on city development: either the strong formal and spatial framework hinders change and development and the city becomes a museum (e.g. Riquewihr in Alsace), or the formal and spatial framework is burst open and coherence is lost (e.g. the first phase of Edinburgh New Town). But good development frameworks, though guiding development into a specific form and structure, can be open-ended and speculative themselves, can allow change and adaptation; the historic development of Glasgow clearly demonstrates this.

But the argument misses the point. Any urban development is as good or bad as the process of control. But what we have to do with today is a city that has emerged as a result of many different development phases applying many different approaches of development control. Though up to the First World War city development was largely coherent at least in spatial and structural terms, the subsequent periods have generated a city that is anything but coherent. It seems symptomatic that today we do not generally monitor the impact of urban development projects on the city, on its citizens or on its regional and global environment. If we did, we might realise that many of these projects are single-minded and single-purpose actions that try to solve one specific problem and ignore the fact that they may create several other problems in the process. A thorough analysis of the impact of today's city on its inhabitants and on the regional and global environment tells us that it has become destructive.

The Purpose of This Book

It is undeniable that the city is shaped by economic forces, and that these forces operate today in a global market. It is equally undeniable that the city has never had and will never have a finite form and structure, owing to the necessity to adapt to changing socio-economic conditions. It is also true that, with a few exceptions, most of our bigger cities in the UK and Europe no longer have an expanding but a stable or shrinking population (though this change seems to be counteracted by the steady increase in the number of smaller households demanding a substantial amount of new accommodation).

But why should these characteristics of the city render urban planning and design superfluous? All arguments supporting a free-for-all development process seem to assume that the form and structure of a city do not matter, and such an assumption is highly questionable. There is, as will be demonstrated later, a clear interrelationship between the spatial, physical and structural characteristics of a city and its functional, socio-economic and environmental qualities or deficiencies. It is therefore unacceptable for urban development to be left to chance; it must be controlled through planning and design frameworks in order to make sure that the city and city region, at any stage of their development, work well, are people-friendly and have a positive environmental impact.

The city's form and structure have for several decades been the target of much destructive development. The impact on the city of garden suburb development during the 1920s and 1930s and of comprehensive development during the 1950s, 1960s and early 1970s has been serious: in the first period the city started to sprawl well beyond the development of previous suburbanisation, in the second it lost much of its historical substance and with it the continuity of its development pattern.

The enterprise culture, which inspired *laissez-faire* attitudes and approaches during the 1980s and early 1990s, has led to even more amorphous growth and remodelling of many of our cities and with it the erosion of the quality of urban space. These physical changes were accompanied by social and economic changes. Many of today's cities have a growing number of under-privileged people forming an 'underclass', people who have no part at all to play in the enterprise culture. Almost all our cities have a zoned land-use pattern which is inadequate (or even destructive) in functional terms, have low-density, sprawling and imageless suburban and peripheral areas as the result of uncontrolled or badly co-ordinated development, and have a physical and spatial structure which not only, in smaller or larger part, is chaotic, ill-functioning, unattractive, stressful and dangerous but also embodies a heavy and increasingly destructive burden on the cities' regional and global environments.

The survival-threatening characteristics of the city and city region can no longer be ignored, and it is vital that ways of sustainable urban living be adopted and that suitable forms and structures of the city and city region be found and put into practice in order to promote this end. It is time to recognise that many of the problems of the city are actually the result of its inadequate structure and form, its distribution of population, its patterns of land use and its systems of transport, all of which are interdependent. City and city region need more than ever to be planned and designed to achieve a truly sustainable urban development. Certainly, the important role economic forces play in the city must be recognised. But these forces must operate *for* rather than *against* the city, and the way in which they manifest themselves in physical, spatial, structural and land-use terms must be guided into forms that enhance rather than destroy the city's quality and identity as a place for people.

It should already have become quite obvious that this book is not primarily focused on aesthetic qualities of urban form – important as these may be when designing individual urban spaces and important as they are to generate a legible and imageable city. The book puts forward an argument for a future city that works well and is people- and environment-friendly. It investigates the formal and structural problems of today's city; and the worlds 'form' and 'formal' refer frequently to physical rather than aesthetic characteristics of the city. The book investigates, and demonstrates the application of, models that might help achieve a better city and city region.

As many of the problems have to do with the city's overall structure and its relationship to the countryside, the role of physical planning and urban design must inevitably be expanded beyond individual urban spaces to the city's districts, the city at large and to its regional hinterland.

Needless to say, improving the city's form and structure is a very long and incremental process, very much like the ongoing city development but governed by strategic development frameworks the major principles of which are adhered to over a long period of time. This book is not at all, therefore, calling for another comprehensive development approach but, on the contrary, advocates a slow but steady process of change, over a period of say 50 or more years, to avoid social and environmental upheaval and to maintain control over the process and what it achieves. Urban change in such a slow but controlled process does not call for large-scale investment over and above that typical for an ongoing development process but for the direction of investment and projects into areas of priority development. Furthermore, rather than being dictated from the top, this process should involve the local communities, which must be given the right and the chance to shape their own environment within the common rules set by the strategic development framework.

The main vehicle for the demonstration of urban design intervention at these levels is the city of Glasgow, not because this city is in a bad state (there are many cities with worse problems, and in the last quarter of this century Glasgow has done a lot to improve its image if not its structure and form) but because Glasgow has been the focus of attention for quite some years and because information on it is readily available.

The purpose of structuring and restructuring proposals for the city and conurbation of Glasgow is not to put forward workable solutions to the city's problems (though, if adopted, if not as a whole then in parts, these proposals might well achieve a better city); Glasgow is the medium, not the message. The approaches and design models are developed as exemplification of the argument about a people- and environment-friendly city, one that works well. The structural and formal (physical) changes suggested are, of course, place specific because they respond to a particular city and to particular characteristics of that city. But the ideas and principles of a 'good' urban structure and organisational form as applied to Glasgow are, I believe, generally valid and implementable in other cities with different physical and locational characteristics, and comparisons of regeneration plans of other cities will be used to demonstrate this.

Part One: The Current Debate About the Sustainable City

The first part of this book focuses on the current debate about a sustainable city form and structure.

Chapter 1

This chapter first defines what urban design is or what it should be, concluding that such 'design' is not a discipline in its own right but – like 'analysis', 'planning', 'forecasting', 'image creating', 'evaluating' and so on – an operational component of all disciplines involved in urban development: urban planning, urban landscape design, city engineering, traffic planning and architectural design. Then an analysis of the deficiencies of today's city leads to an expansion of the argument that today the city needs strategic planning and design more than ever, and the levels at which urban design has to operate are defined.

Chapter 2

There follows a summary of the ongoing 'sustainable city' discussion and of the different types of city models suggested as being more or less sustainable. It will become clear that the debate is confused and inconclusive overall, largely owing to the fact that researchers and writers frequently do not clearly specify the structural, spatial or formal characteristics of the city models

they actually talk about. Nevertheless, this comparison of opinions leads to a list of generally accepted sustainability criteria which are formalised so that they can be used as the basis for the evaluation of different city models.

Chapter 3

On the basis of the key sustainability criteria the microstructure of the city or settlement is then investigated and a recommendation is made to introduce, or (better) re-introduce, a hierarchy of provision centres and links between them. This is followed by an examination of the macro-structure of different city models. A comparison of their areas and overall dimensions as well as their performance regarding the sustainability criteria leads to the conclusion that each model offers a different range of advantages and disadvantages, and that the choice between them may depend upon their overall population size, their suitability for public transport and, most importantly, their applicability in existing cities and city regions.

Part Two: Application of the Model Urban Structure to Glasgow

In Part Two of the book, what has been learned from the debate about a sustainable city form and structure is applied to an existing conurbation, that of Glasgow.

Chapter 4

First Glasgow's major development stages are reviewed and the city's qualities and efficiencies are summarised. This chapter does not attempt a thorough historical account (which has been provided elsewhere) but seeks to portray the city's major characteristics in order to enable those not so familiar with the city to follow the development of a macro- and micro-structure which might help achieve a better-functioning city and city region.

Chapter 5

Then the existing macro-structure of the city region and conurbation is studied. It is concluded that, owing to the existing fragmentation of the urban fabric, of the various city models analysed in Part One the 'polycentric net' is the most suitable. A macro-structure for the city region and the city having been established, the existing microstructure of the conurbation of Glasgow is investigated and an attempt is made to define, within the conurbation, neighbourhoods, districts and towns with their respective provision centres. This investigation results in a plausible structure not only for centres of services and facilities of different capacity but also for nodes of public transport systems of different capacity.

The conclusion of the exercise of generating a better structure is that both the specifically applied macro-structure – a form of decentralised concentration – and the generally applicable micro-structure – a hierarchy of provision centres and linkages – fit well into the region and conurbation of Glasgow. They reinforce – without any major structural changes but by enhancing the existing structural properties – a network of development entities of different sizes and complexities that is highly flexible and well linked with the open country.

Chapter 6

After the applicability of macro- and micro-structure has been established on city region and conurbation level, several rather different urban districts are briefly investigated and the micro-structure is applied there, again with success.

Epilogue

The final section investigates the political, social, professional and educational changes required to make strategic urban design operational at the city and regional levels. Some of these changes will undoubtedly appear to be quite radical, but for the survival of the city as well as its regional and global hinterland no change, if vital, is too radical.

References

Alexander, C., Neis, H., Anninou, A. and King, I. (1987) *A New Theory of Urban Design*, Oxford University Press, Oxford.

Tibbalds, F. (1992) *Making People-Friendly Towns*, Longman, London.

Venturi, R., Scott Brown, D. and Izenour, S. (1972) *Learning from Las Vegas*, MIT Press, Cambridge, Mass.

Part One

The Current Debate about the Sustainable City

What Urban Design Is and Why it is so Important Today

Urban design is a rather unfortunate term describing greatly confused responsibilities of people supposedly involved in the design of the city's 'public realm'. Urban design in the UK is a professional hybrid, a relatively recent invention intended to mediate between the responsibilities of urban and regional planners and architects.

A fruitful discussion of the enhancement of the physical form and spatial structure of the city must be based on a much clearer understanding of what urban design is or should be, what responsibilities it has or should have, and what its levels of intervention with the city are or should be. This first chapter develops a definition of urban design that results from an understanding of some problematic characteristics of form and structure of the city region, the city and its districts, all of which are believed to require urgent improvement.

1.1 What Urban Design is or What it Should Be

There seem to be as many definitions of urban design in the UK as there are urban designers. I shall not go into a detailed investigation, which has been done elsewhere (Madanipour, 1996), but almost all these definitions see urban design as bridging the gap between planning and architecture. In the 1960s these two disciplines 'most immediately concerned with the design of the urban environment' (Gosling and Maitland, 1984, p. 7) decided to split. They developed separate university courses, with planning focusing on land-use patterns and socio-economic issues and architecture on the design of buildings. The gap of responsibilities between the two disciplines soon became apparent and urban design came into existence as an attempt to cover issues for which neither planning nor architecture claimed responsibility: the design of public spaces.

Urban Design In The UK: The Theory

The frequently adopted definition of urban design is that it is

> concerned with the physical form of the public realm over a limited physical area of the city and that it therefore lies between the two well-established design scales of architecture, which is concerned with the physical form of the private realm of the individual building, and town and regional planning, which is concerned with the organisation of the public realm in its wider context.

(Gosling and Maitland, 1984, p. 9)

There are problems with this definition. One is that it does not seem to recognise that much of what is called the 'public realm', the city's public streets and squares, is actually physically bounded by elements of the 'private realm', by private buildings. The design of streets and squares cannot ignore the design features of those private buildings that form the edges of these spaces. Urban design, though primarily responsible for the design of public streets and squares, must therefore set at least some rules for the design of those elements of the private realm that are involved in the formation of the public realm. Similarly, parts of the city's public realm, the public buildings and monuments, are designed not by the urban designer but by the architect. And this makes matters more complicated because inevitably the urban designer's responsibility overlaps at the micro-scale of operations with that of the architect, as the architect's does with that of the urban designer.

Another problem with this definition is that it does not specify what the 'public realm' is. In the traditional city the public realm, which Leon Krier called 'Res Publica', includes all public monuments, halls, memorials and public works the vertical features of which shape the city's skyline, as well as all major public streets and squares that link these urban components or front them (see Papadakis, 1984, pp. 40–1). These components of the public realm are embedded within the fabric of the private realm, called by Leon Krier 'Res (Economica) Privata', which provides accommodation for living, production, administration, commerce, storage, health care, defence and security, and which, in relationship to the public realm, is in the traditional city subordinate to the public realm and forms the city's horizontal mass *(Fig. 1.01)*.

This distinction is useful and illustrates that not all public spaces are of the same importance; some may have only local, others district- or even city-wide significance. And the same differentiation of importance must be made for urban monuments. Urban design should respond to the distinction between more or less important components of the city, between those that are long-lasting, structure-generating and form-giving for the city (or urban districts) at large and others that may be modified as a consequence of socio-economic changes and are therefore less significant with regard to the city's form and structure. But if this distinction is adopted then the restriction of the responsibility of urban design to a 'limited physical area of the city', as defined above, becomes rather problematic because it precludes urban design from having a holistic view of the city, which then only urban planning would have. But adopting a holistic view makes matters even more complicated because it causes the urban designer's responsibility to overlap at the macro-scale of operations with that of the urban planner.

Consequently, the amenability of urban design can neither be restricted to the elements of the public realm only, much of which is bounded by elements of the private realm, nor be restricted to a limited physical area of the city because then it would be ineffective in the shaping of the city's and its districts' physical form and skyline and their spatial structure. Urban design therefore does not fit neatly in between the responsibilities and activities of urban and regional planning and architecture; its responsibilities overlap considerably with the concerns of both disciplines.

Urban Design In The UK: The Practice

The run-down state of many of the UK's cities' public streets and squares, even those of major importance, seems to indicate that there is very little care for, let alone design of, the public realm *(Fig. 1.02)*. In contrast, a city like Barcelona, for instance, illustrates a great concern for the quality of public streets and squares which are co-ordinated to form an urban network and designed and executed to a high standard *(Fig. 1.03)*. There are always notable exceptions, but generally there seems to be very little urban design of that kind in the UK's cities.

Because of the lack of a common definition, there are many different kinds of urban projects which are claimed to fall into the category of urban design. There are many theoretical but rather fewer real examples of urban design which deal with development pattern, spatial structure and physical form of specific urban areas, mostly relatively small in dimensions, very much in tune with the generally adopted view of the nature of urban design and focusing on the improvement of the public realm. Typical examples of such design projects emerged, for instance, from the 'Quality in Town and

1–01. The public and the private realm of the city illustrated by the skyline of central Florence

1–02. Byres Road, Glasgow

1–03. Avinguda de Gaudí, Barcelona

Country' Initiative, launched by the Secretary of State in 1994 (DoE, 1994), a key stage of which culminated in the exhibition of 21 case studies from different parts of the UK with the focus on the creation of a sense of place, identity and civic pride through new development (DoE, 1996). Another typical example of this kind of urban design is the plan for the regeneration of the bomb-damaged area in the city centre of Manchester. Manchester City Council promoted an international competition to redefine the city centre and this resulted in a master plan (Manchester Millennium, 1996) and supplementary planning guidance for the area (Manchester City Council, 1996).

Otherwise, many of the other UK projects called urban design fall into two categories: they are either architectural master-planning, i.e. the design of large-scale and almost exclusively private architectural projects rather than the design of public streets and squares, or they are the largely cosmetic treatment of individual public spaces. Two examples can easily illustrate this.

The Canary Wharf project in London's Docklands is a large architectural project developed on the basis of a master plan for a group of buildings along a central axis, designed in minute detail for one developer by a small number of architectural firms *(Fig. 1.04)*. The major central axis is not really a public street but, rather like the mall in a shopping complex, private and accordingly not freely accessible to the public. This project

1–04. Canary Wharf, London: master plan model

(a)

(b)

1–05. *Royal Exchange Square, Glasgow. (a) The square before refurbishment; (b) the square after refurbishment in 1997*

demonstrates international speculative forces at work. To express their ranking in the hierarchy of importance of such forces, the project applies a monumental scale and architectural language for publicly less significant elements of the private economic realm. We may have become used to the 'cathedrals of commerce' in the 'city', but what remains frequently unexplored in such large-scale architectural projects – and Canary Wharf is no exception – is their relationship to the urban context. They frequently fail to link into and enhance the structure, morphology and use pattern of an urban district. The fact that many such projects ignore the urban context and the people living and working around them illustrates the 'architectural' and private nature of such development rather than the concern for the public realm and the quality of an urban district for the inhabitants.

The other kind of 'urban design' practised in the UK is the cosmetic treatment of existing streets and squares, limited betterment of hard and soft landscaping as demonstrated, for instance, in the 'Great Streets' project in Glasgow *(Fig. 1.05a, b)*. Useful as such improvement may be for a particular public space, it is in the end fully effective only if it represents part of a much wider plan, say of the promotion of the network of important public spaces of an entire district, without which it remains an

isolated event. Though this point, which will be returned to later, is rather obvious, urban design in the UK that actually deals with the public realm is generally limited to individual and disparate spaces: it improves a particular place but very rarely has a strategic dimension as long as it fails to be part of a district- or city-wide advancement plan.

Projects of both categories may indeed achieve important local development and advancement but, because they are not co-ordinated and orchestrated, they do not add up to more than the sum of their parts and the city remains a more or less chaotic patchwork *(Fig. 1.06)*.

Urban Design in Other European Countries and Cities

In the UK, planning has largely abolished the responsibility for the physical form of the city and its districts. Development control, the responsibility of planning, is generally based on two-dimensional structure plans focusing on land-use patterns and socio-economic issues, and predominantly two-dimensional local plans dealing with problems and opportunities of a specific urban area or district. Local plans may be supported by design guidelines but they are usually general rather than place specific; that is, they frequently do not distinguish between more and less important components of the public and private realm.

It is interesting to observe that in the German-speaking countries of Europe, for instance, urban planning has remained much closer to architecture than in the UK. Many, if not the majority, of planning courses remain integrated in schools of architecture, with planning at such schools being seen as a field of specialisation growing out of an architectural education. Therefore it is not surprising that in these countries development and control of the physical form of the city remains an integrated part of urban development control (see Pantel, 1994). In addition to structure and local plans, they operate with what they call *Bebauungspläne*, plans regulating not only the land use but also the built form of streets, squares, districts and the city *(Fig. 1.07)*. It might be appropriate to call such plans 'urban design frameworks'.

The degree to which such *Bebauungspläne* regulate the physical form of development depends on the importance of individual places or districts for the city. Design rules may be stringent for significant places and areas, prescribing even small details of physical development, maybe including the detailing of facades and the formation of the roofs of buildings; or they may be rather relaxed for less significant places, prescribing only the overall massing of development or leaving it entirely open and restricting perhaps only the height of development. A set of such *Bebauungspläne* may

1–06. The Scottish Exhibition and Conference Centre, Glasgow, seen across what was the Garden Festival site

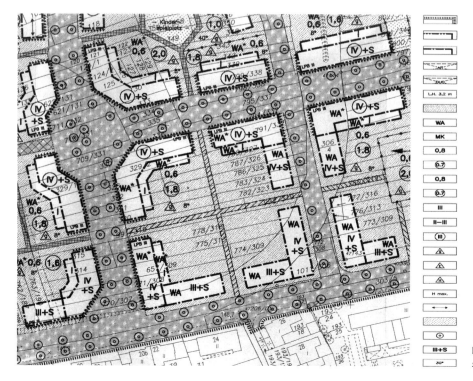

1–07. Example of a Bebauungsplan: *a housing scheme in Frankfurt am Main*

therefore be orchestrated to control the important features, places and districts of a city and to grant relative freedom for development in the less important areas. Very frequently details of *Bebauungspläne* are the result of design competitions as the well-documented Berlin IBA experience demonstrates (IBA Berlin, AR September 1984; AR April 1987; IBA 1984, 1981). And whereas in the UK structure and local plans represent guidelines, those in the German-speaking countries, including the *Bebauungspläne*, once passed by local council or government, have legal status and represent a very powerful means of urban development control.

The Question of Over- or Under-regulating Urban Development

One may argue that over-regulating urban development by means of something like a *Bebauungsplan* will not only be counter-productive in development terms, for instance scaring away developers, but will generate a mediocre, if not monotonous, urban environment, lacking formal variety and design ingenuity which is stifled by excessively tight rules *(Fig. 1.08a)*. Well, this may be true in some cases, but compare the results of under-regulating urban development, which invites idiosyncratic projects and brings little if any co-ordination *(Fig. 1.08b)*.

Any approach is only as good as its implementation, and the question is not whether or not there should be any urban design frameworks for the co-ordination of the physical form of urban development but what form of urban design framework and what degree of co-ordination is applied and for which areas or places in the city. The city as a physical entity is composed of many different elements which relate to each other functionally and spatially. Just as a pile of parts becomes a well-functioning car only when arranged in the right functional and spatial order, so disparate urban elements create a 'good' (i.e. a well-functioning, people- and environment-friendly) city only if they are orchestrated in an appropriate functional and spatial order which enables the elements to interact effectively.

The functional and spatial order which orchestrates urban elements either is the result of commonly accepted development rules and patterns, the result of a 'social logic of space' (Hillier and Hanson, 1984), perhaps, which regulates the development of the traditional city, or is the result of urban design. Without such an order, however derived, the city does not function effectively.

The Question of the Scale and Extent of Urban Design Frameworks and Interventions

As I have already indicated, urban design is said to be concerned with the physical form and structure of an area of limited size, perhaps 'half a mile [0.8 km] square' (Banham, 1976, p. 130). Many in the UK seem to agree with this limitation of scale of urban design intervention and support this with the argument that since cities never have a finite physical form and structure, as they develop and change continuously, it is futile to develop urban design frameworks for the city at large. It may indeed be true that the city never has a finite form unless it has become a museum, but it does have a temporary overall form at any stage of its development. History tells us that a 'good' city evolves on the basis of local characteristics and design principles, not by mere chance. History also tells us that 'good' urban structures and forms – those that enable and enhance urban activities, improve on the well-being of the citizens and create a balanced relationship with their local and global environment – are generally preserved and therefore long-lasting because they function well and express their and their citizens' history, collective memory, values and beliefs and pride.

With today's rapidly changing socio-economic conditions the city changes rapidly as well. If this change occurs at the level of the private (economic) realm without affecting the dominance of the long-lasting public realm then the city maintains the identity generated by the public realm, and it continues to be recognised as a unique, imageable place by both its citizens and visitors alike. If rapid changes occur in both the private and the public realm then the city may continue to work well in functional terms but will lose its imageability and identity and the citizens may lose the ability to foster a sense of belonging. The image, the mental map, people form of their city is the result of use-patterns and of long-lasting physical (i.e. formal and structural) characteristics that make, for instance, Florence Florence and Glasgow Glasgow, and these characteristics are the result of a specific skyline, of a specific spatial structure, of specific use and development patterns and specific places and monuments.

Though for some a rapidly changing city, like Tokyo, may seem a highly appropriate urban model for the twenty-first century, it does not have a lasting identity and is therefore likely to fail to provide the emotional security and the sense of belonging possessed by those who live in places with a unique physiognomy and identity. A 'good' city, at least in those parts of the world in which cities have a history, has long-lasting, image-generating elements, form and structure as well as the ability to adapt to changing needs and socio-economic conditions. It is the task of urban design to make sure that the image-providing characteristics of the city do not change, or change only very slowly, and that the general urban fabric can adapt continuously without interfering with the quality of the city's public realm. And this can be achieved only if the city is seen as an entity. Restricting urban design to smaller urban areas is rendering it ineffective for such a task.

(a)

(b)

1–08. *Illustrations of over- and under-regulated urban development. (a) Bofill's Antigon, Montpellier; (b) the Docklands, London*

Summary Definition of Urban Design

Any physical part of the city has a form, and the orchestration of such parts generates a specific urban form and structure. Any physical part of the city is accordingly designable, and so is the orchestration of these parts to form streets, squares, urban fabric, monuments, a skyline. Though the form and structure of the traditional city may have evolved in a slow and incremental process without formal planning and design, it evolved on the basis of commonly understood and accepted development patterns. Today, so many non-local forces are shaping the city – forces that frequently do not even know the specific cities in which they are at work – that rules and patterns need to be introduced in the form of

development and design frameworks which must be based on the city's particular history, culture, location and topography in order to safeguard its identity.

Such frameworks are generally understood to be the responsibility of the urban planner and designer. But this is the view of current practice rather than a response to the actual nature of the planning and design process. Like planning, forecasting, image-creating, evaluating, etc., designing is one of the *many* activities that is, or should be, the responsibility of *all* people and disciplines involved in urban development and its control. The reason for this is that any urban development plan will eventually manifest itself in a physical end result, a product, which needs to be shaped, designed. This shaping and designing should not be an afterthought because design that is applied to a pre-existing and pre-developed plan is a cosmetic operation, indeed 'the kind of magic dust you sprinkle on at the end' (Tibbalds, 1992, p. 4), which cannot at that stage contribute to the shaping of the plan. The design of a product should be conceived in parallel with a conjecture that sets into motion a process which will eventually result in the realisation of the product. Designing the city should therefore *not* be left to a 'specialist', the 'urban designer'. The interactive process of developing an urban plan and land-use pattern and designing an appropriate urban form and structure should not be separated into different disciplinary responsibilities but should be the responsibility of, and should be carried out by, whoever is involved in the generation of plans for urban development. From this it follows that urban design is not and should not be a discipline in its own right, somewhere between planning and architecture. Designing the city or parts of it should be an operational component of all disciplines involved in urban development, from urban planning, traffic and infrastructure planning and engineering to urban landscaping and architecture.

Based on urban development and regeneration plans, design sets, or should set, the framework, the rules and guidelines for the form and orchestration of the city's physical parts and by doing so it creates the city's physical form and structure. Design is accordingly responsible not only for individual public spaces and monuments – and on this level is an activity quite close to if not a component of architecture – but also for urban districts and for the city at large and its relationship to the hinterland – and at that level is a component of urban and regional planning, traffic and infrastructure planning, and urban landscaping. This constitutes the *process* of urban design.

Regarding the *product* of urban design, guidelines and frameworks have to make sure that the city has two fundamentally important characteristics: to be both *imageable* and *adaptable*. Urban design must consolidate and enhance the city's public realm in such a way that it preserves, improves or creates a long-lasting image of a city and its urban districts that are clearly identifiable as being unique. In parallel, urban design must enable and enhance the continuous process of adaptation of the city's private realm to changing needs and aspirations of its citizens in their changing socio-economic conditions. The design of the public realm is vitally important for the quality of the city's form and structure and needs to be carefully controlled. Except where it forms an important part of the public realm, the urban fabric of the private realm must be much less regulated and free to adapt, but this does not mean that it is inevitably formless, ugly or chaotic. The private realm should also be well designed; its development must, however, be subordinated to the image-giving public realm so that it does not interfere with or even destroy the city's imageable form and structure.

To summarise, urban design as defined here is an activity that should be shared by and be the responsibility of all those involved in and accountable for urban development and regeneration. Its task is to improve by design the city region's, the city's and its districts' physical form and structure: the network of important public streets and squares, and individual spaces. Such a much wider interpretation of the nature and role of design in urban development has considerable consequences for professional education and practice. This point will be taken up again towards the end of this book.

1.2 Why Urban Design is Needed More Than Ever Today

Today most people live in cities and conurbations, and their population is growing world-wide. According to the World Resource Institute and the Institute for Environment and Development, in 1986 and 1988–9 the urban population of Europe was 71.6% and that of the UK 92.1% of the respective total population (Elkin and McLaren with Hillman, 1991, p. 5). The city is accordingly the place that influences and shapes the life of a vast number of people. For this reason alone the quality of the city is of paramount importance. This in turn highlights the significance of planning and designing the city.

There are other and even more significant reasons why planning and designing the city is so important today. The most crucial one is that current urban development and urban living are today regarded by many as ultimately unsustainable because of the destructive burden they place on the environment. One of the causes for this destructive influence is believed to be the city's very form and structure, which urgently require improvement. This in turn highlights the vital role urban planning and design have to play in a process that attempts to rescue the global environment and with it the hinterland upon which the city utterly depends. It is therefore essential to spell out the significant contribution urban planning and design can and should make towards sustainable urban development and living by improving the city's form and structure and, as a consequence, making the city a more people-friendly place and reducing its destructive environmental impact.

Urban Design Can Help Enhance the City's Advantages

It is questionable whether so many people would live in cities if city life did not offer at least some advantages over living in the country. The city's most important advantages are often said to be that it offers choice, an exciting lifestyle; it provides access to services and facilities; it has stimulating features and represents an

1–09. Las Ramblas, Barcelona

intellectual challenge; it offers comradeship; and, most obviously and importantly, it offers workplaces *(Fig. 1.09)*.

However, all cities are different and some offer their citizens more advantages than do others. It is the main objective of good urban planning and design to create new advantages or enhance the existing advantages a 'good' city has to offer. A list of such advantages can be constructed by following Maslow's hierarchy of human needs (Maslow, 1954). The various demands on the city thus derived form an excellent basis for the measurement of the quality of a city by establishing what levels of human needs and aspirations it is able to satisfy.

- On the basic level, a 'good' city provides for all the physical needs of its citizens: a place to live and work, a reasonable income, education and training, transport and the possibility to communicate, access to services and facilities.

- Beyond this, a 'good' city offers safety, security and protection, a visually and functionally ordered and controlled environment free of pollution, noise, accidents, crime.

- A 'good' city offers, furthermore, a conducive social environment. It is a place where people have their roots and children have their friends; it enables the individual to be part of a community and provides the feeling of belonging to a place, to a territory.

- Then a 'good' city has an appropriate image, a good reputation and prestige; it gives people a sense of confidence and strength, a status and dignity.

- Even higher up in the hierarchy of human needs, a 'good' city offers people a chance to be

creative, to shape their personal space and to express themselves; it offers communities the chance to shape their districts and neighbourhoods according to their needs and aspirations.

- And finally, a 'good' city is well designed, aesthetically pleasing, physically imageable; a 'good' city is a place of culture and a work of art.

It goes without saying that urban design on its own cannot achieve a city that has all these properties, many of which depend upon social and economic conditions which need to be planned for. But design can shape the physical properties of the city and its districts in such a way that they can become the places for the fulfilment of people's wants and requirements.

History shows that the city has never provided for all the needs of all of its people. There have always been some people who could 'live the good life' which Aristotle, in *Politics*, saw as the reason why people move into and stay in cities. But there have always been some people for whom the city does not provide the good life, and in today's city the number of those living a miserable life seems to be larger then ever. Yet there are voices that tell us that cities are good for us, or at least that cities could be good for us, and for all of us 'if strategic planning were restored, population densities maintained, public transport preferred to private cars, and urban street housing re-established and improved upon' (Sherlock, 1991, p. 20). The suggested improvements would undoubtedly provide some of the essential qualities of a 'good' city as defined above, and they highlight the importance of urban planning and design.

Urban Design Can Help Diminish or Eliminate the City's Disadvantages

Clearly, the city also has, and has always had, disadvantages: it is frequently overcrowded, though not necessarily today in the UK; it is dirty, noisy, polluted, congested *(Fig. 1.10)*. Furthermore, living in close proximity to one another may infringe upon people's privacy and freedom, may deprive them of a truly personal space, indoor and outdoor. However, as a result of continuous urbanisation and, during recent decades, the lack of strategic urban planning and urban design to channel urbanisation into appropriate forms and structures, the city's disadvantages have today become grave: it has started to destroy the very hinterland upon which it depends.

The City is No Longer Contained

Planning has reflected over the past century or so the principles of zoning, of the low-density monofunctional garden suburb and later of functionalism. As a consequence the city has been allowed to grow

1–10. Busy boulevard in Paris

without limitation of its size and population. First the railway and later the car provided the required mobility and the city lost its compactness. Few attempts were made to appraise the consequences of potentially limitless urban growth in terms of distances and journeys, energy consumption and pollution, congestion of roads and increasingly inaccessible central facilities. And the larger the city grew in size and population, the more congestion resulted, and the more the suburban exodus accelerated (Mumford, 1984, p. 584).

There is a counter-movement which started towards the end of the nineteenth century with people like Peter Kropotkin and Ebenezer Howard. The latter put forward a new physical form and structure for urban growth which would reintroduce a balanced and ecological relationship between the city – of limited size and population – and the countryside – of sufficient size to support the city with all necessary goods and material – as well as a balance between the varied functions of the city, again as a result of the strict limitation of its size and population. 'If the city was to maintain its life-maintaining functions for its inhabitants, it must in its own right exhibit the organic self-control and self-containment of any other organism' (Mumford, 1984, p. 587). However, Howard's model of a 'town-cluster', which we shall study in more detail later, was not able to halt the growth and suburbanisation of our cities, perhaps mainly because the rate of expansion of the city in terms of land, industrial development and population was so high that control and containment would have been difficult (Mumford, 1984, p. 596).

Today the European city has, with a few notable exceptions, entered a post-industrial phase and its population is stable if not shrinking. What we have inherited, and are still continuing to develop further, is a city of huge dimensions that has by far outgrown its population. Many of the city's workplaces, services and facilities are concentrated in a single core. The centre has lost its attraction as a place for living and people have moved into surrounding suburban housing areas and high-rise dormitories lacking any history, diversity of activities, cultural and other forms of infrastructure and a recognisable individuality with which the citizens can identify. Retail and other uses followed people into the suburbs and peripheral areas, endangering the viability of the city centre. The question has been asked whether we can speak of 'cities' or whether we must think in terms of 'urban areas' which 'negate the concept of the city itself: they become "post-urban" phenomena, far removed from the traditional image of the pre-industrial and even 19th century city' (Commission of the European Communities, 1990, p. 6).

The City is Zoned and Obliges People to Travel

First as a result of industrialisation, then because of the availability of mechanised transport (in the form of railways and later the car) and now because current planning often still reflects principles of functionalism, the city is zoned according to uses and this generates the need to travel from one zone to another. Of specific significance is the concentration of city-wide activities and facilities in the city centre and of housing in suburban and peripheral dormitory places. With a low average population density public transport is not really viable, not only because it has been underfunded for decades but simply because in the suburbs and peripheral estates it cannot target a sufficient number of people to make it function economically. Therefore the car remains the more convenient and often cheaper means of inner-city transport for those who can afford it, but the ever-increasing density of vehicular traffic generates more and more pollution, congestion and stress in central areas. The problem with pollution may be solved, partly or wholly, with new emission-free fuels, but the problem of congestion remains.

During much recent political history the trend towards a car-dependent city was supported. Only in the past few years has central government in the UK made a U-turn and is now suggesting that in the city priority must be given to public transport (DoE and DoT, 1994). What has not yet been fully recognised, however, is that the objective to achieve a well-functioning, comfortable and economically viable network of public transport requires a review of land-use policies, population density and the form and structure of the city.

The City is Socially Stratified

The development of use-zones and specifically the concentration of public housing in suburban and peripheral estates – often with poor housing stock and landscaping, far from urban facilities and poorly served by public transport – makes such areas unable to fulfil all of people's needs and, as a result, they become socially

exclusive if not 'the slums of the late 1970s and 1980s' (Commission of the European Communities, 1990, p. 24). Those with higher incomes who can afford mobility and higher house prices move into advantaged areas in and outside the city *(Fig. 1.11a)*. Those with lower and specifically those with no income who cannot afford mobility and higher house prices or depend upon the provision of social housing become trapped in disadvantaged areas of the city *(Fig. 1.11b)*.

As a result, the city's socio-economic stratification has been exacerbated to a considerable degree; there are now underprivileged areas with all the signs of deprivation including unemployment, lack of education and skills, ill health, drug abuse, vandalism and crime. In such areas, where people are physically isolated from and deprived of the economic, social, commercial and cultural life of the city, social unrest has become part of everyday life. A city with such a degree of social stratification is not sustainable. The only way to solve this problem is to make the city's districts more equitable.

The City has a Destructive Environmental Impact

The city's negative environmental impact has increased to an extent that now threatens the regional and global

(a)

(b)

1–11. Examples of housing for the privileged and underprivileged in Paris. (a) High-rise high-density housing at La Défense; (b) low-rise high-density housing on the Ile de la Seine

environment. The city's hinterland that provides it with food, raw materials and energy is no longer the countryside surrounding it; now the city draws resources from all over the globe. The city has become the largest user and waster of raw materials and energy and the largest producer of liquid, solid and gaseous waste. The degree of depletion of raw materials and of pollution of land, air and water is truly unsustainable because if not reduced it will eventually destroy the very hinterland the city depends upon. Much of this has been widely documented in the literature (see Girardet, 1992; Elkin and McLaren with Hillman, 1991; Commission of the European Communities, 1990) and is the basis of today's intensive debate about a sustainable city form which will be reviewed in the following chapter.

The Role of Urban Design

As the struggle of Los Angeles with pollution and congested roads demonstrates, technological and scientific solutions may generate new and clean fuel, effective transport, continuous and renewable energy (*Fig. 1.12*) and the like, and behavioural changes may lead people away from a throw-away approach (a linear metabolism) to recycling and reuse of materials (a cyclic metabolism). But all these efforts need to be supported by an improvement – through urban design – of the physical characteristics of the city so that its destructive environmental impact is minimised, as proposed in a BBC2 *Horizon* programme, 'California Dreaming', shown on 11 February 1991.

It is the task of urban planning and design to enable and enhance the city's advantages and to minimise if not eliminate the city's disadvantages. The city must become more equitable; it must provide every citizen with a fair share of its advantages. On the other hand the city needs to be shaped so that a considerable reduction of noise and pollution is achieved, so that mobility is possible without congestion of roads and without pollu-

1–12. Wind turbines in Rotterdam

tion, so that planned and spontaneous communication is possible, and so that people enjoy a high level of privacy and freedom. A 'good' city combines the central qualities of the traditional city – culture, exchange of ideas, a creative atmosphere, the availability of retail outlets, services and facilities – with the qualities of the suburb – privacy, solitude, freedom, quietness, good air, gardens, parks and promenades – without taking on the unsustainable characteristics of many of today's suburban and peripheral areas – single use, low density, sprawl, monotony and car dependency.

The main objective of the first part of this book is to review the debate about a sustainable city form and structure, to formulate, as a consequence of this debate, a set of sustainability criteria for urban design, and to analyse the form and structure of city models that, I suggest, are more sustainable than today's city.

1.3 The Levels of Urban Design Interventions

To enhance the city's advantages and to minimise its disadvantages requires urban design to operate on a level way beyond that of individual spaces or areas of restricted size, as suggested in the definition of urban design at the beginning of this chapter. Urban design is therefore not only 'design of the public realm', of the city's most important public spaces and monuments, but has to deal with the physical form and structure of the city region, of the city at large, and of its districts (*Fig. 1.13*). Only after having generated development frameworks at these levels and in this hierarchical order (city region – city – city districts), can design effectively deal with individual urban spaces.

Strategic Urban Design on City Regional Level

Today, the pre-eminent task of design is not to provide cosmetic treatment of individual spaces. As form and structure of the city partially or totally generate some environmental and functional problems and are the physical manifestation of the social and economic stratification of the city, it is the most urgent and essential task of design to contribute on a strategic level to the improvement not only of land-use patterns but of the city region's and the city's form and structure. Design frameworks at this level will develop a balanced and functional relationship of the city with its hinterland, will generate a spatial and formal structure for the city's districts in their interaction and interrelatedness, and will set the conditions for design on the next lower level of the city districts.

Strategic Urban Design on City District Level

Another urgent task of design is to contribute to the enhancement of the quality of urban districts, many of which are today monotonous, single-use areas and dor-

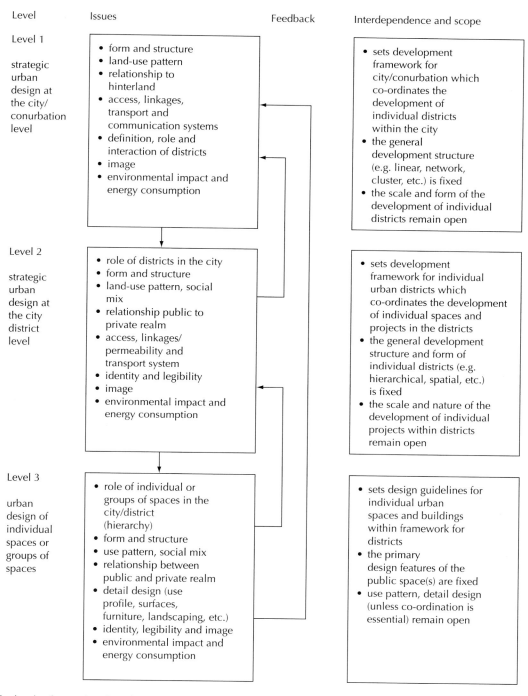

Level	Issues	Feedback	Interdependence and scope
Level 1 strategic urban design at the city/ conurbation level	• form and structure • land-use pattern • relationship to hinterland • access, linkages, transport and communication systems • definition, role and interaction of districts • image • environmental impact and energy consumption		• sets development framework for city/conurbation which co-ordinates the development of individual districts within the city • the general development structure (e.g. linear, network, cluster, etc.) is fixed • the scale and form of the development of individual districts remain open
Level 2 strategic urban design at the city district level	• role of districts in the city • form and structure • land-use pattern, social mix • relationship public to private realm • access, linkages/ permeability and transport system • identity and legibility • image • environmental impact and energy consumption		• sets development framework for individual urban districts which co-ordinates the development of individual spaces and projects in the districts • the general development structure and form of individual districts (e.g. hierarchical, spatial, etc.) is fixed • the scale and nature of the development of individual projects within districts remain open
Level 3 urban design of individual spaces or groups of spaces	• role of individual or groups of spaces in the city/district (hierarchy) • form and structure • use pattern, social mix • relationship between public and private realm • detail design (use profile, surfaces, furniture, landscaping, etc.) • identity, legibility and image • environmental impact and energy consumption		• sets design guidelines for individual urban spaces and buildings within framework for districts • the primary design features of the public space(s) are fixed • use pattern, detail design (unless co-ordination is essential) remain open

1–13. The levels of strategic urban design interventions

mitory places. Their form, structure, density, use patterns and generally their role in the city, the degree of equity and the quality of life they provide need to be investigated and in many places dramatically redesigned and improved. It is on this level that design deals with the spatial, formal and structural interrelationship between the public and the private realm and with the generation of design guidelines for both the important public elements of districts and the urban fabric that generates their neutral background or framework.

Urban Design on Level of Individual Spaces

On the lowest level of intervention, design is responsible for the quality of individual public streets and squares and the network of public spaces they form. This is the kind of urban design we are most familiar with in the UK, and this book will therefore not deal with it.

1.4 Summary and Scope for Further Exploration

There are a lot of very good and useful publications discussing and demonstrating urban design of the public realm, of public spaces and monuments in the city and the role public and private buildings play in their definition and identity (Bentley *et al.*, 1985; Broadbent, 1990; Cullen, 1961, 1985; Gosling and Maitland, 1984; Tibbalds, 1992; Trancik, 1986). This book does not need to repeat any of the arguments in these works.

Little, however, is said, discussed and published about urban design at the city district level and not much at all concerning the city and city/region level. Further discussion will therefore concentrate on design on these levels. There will inevitably be many overlaps with planning and other issues, but the discussion will go beyond land-use patterns and focus on the physical form and structure of the city at large and of its districts as a result of demands regarding urban functions, social, economic and environmental conditions as well as the form and image of the city and its towns and districts.

References

Banham, R. (1976) *Megastructure: Urban Futures of the Recent Past*, Thames & Hudson, London.

Bentley, I., Alcock, A., Murrain, P., McGlynn, S. and Smith, G. (1985) *Responsive Environments: A Manual for Designers*, The Architectural Press, London.

Broadbent, G. (1990) *Emerging Concepts of Urban Space Design*, Van Nostrand Reinhold, London.

Commission of the European Communities (1990) *Green Paper on the Urban Environment*, COM(90) 218 final, Brussels.

Cullen, G. (1961) *The Concise Townscape*, The Architectural Press, London.

Cullen, G. (1985) *Townscape*, The Architectural Press, London.

Department of the Environment (1994) *Quality in Town and Country – A Discussion Document*, DoE, London.

Department of the Environment (1996) *Quality in Town and Country – Urban Design Exhibition*, DoE, London.

Department of the Environment and Department of Transport (1994) *Planning Policy Guidance 13: Transport*, HMSO, London.

Elkin, T. and McLaren, D. with Hillman, M. (1991) *Reviving the City: Towards Sustainable Urban Development*, Friends of the Earth, London.

Girardet, H. (1992) *The Gaia Atlas of Cities: New Directions for Sustainable Urban Living*, Gaia Books, London.

Gosling, D. and Maitland, B. (1984) *Concepts of Urban Design*, Academy Editions, London.

Hillier, B. and Hanson, J. (1984) *The Social Logic of Space*, Cambridge University Press, Cambridge.

IBA Berlin, AR No. 1051, September 1984, AR No. 1082, April 1987; Internationale Bauausstellung Berlin 1984, *Die Neubaugebiete: Dokumente Projekte*, Heft 2, Quadriga Verlag, Berlin, 1981.

Madanipour, A. (1996) *Design of Urban Space*, Wiley, New York (chapter 4: comprehensive analysis of definitions of urban design).

Manchester City Council (1996) *Supplementary Planning Guidance for the City Centre Bomb Damaged Area*, Technical Services Department and Manchester Millennium Ltd (City Centre Task Force), Manchester.

Manchester Millennium Ltd (1996) *A Masterplan Framework for the Future*, EDAW in association with Baxters Benoy Simpson BDP, 6 December 1996 update, Manchester.

Maslow, A. (1954) *Motivation and Personality*, Harper & Row, New York.

Mumford, L. (1984) *The City in History*, Penguin Books, Harmondsworth (reprinted; first published in the USA 1961).

Pantel, G. (1994) Design control in German planning, in Punter, J.V. (ed.) *Design Control in Europe, Built Environment*, Vol. 20, No. 2, Alexandrine Press, Oxford.

Papadakis, A. (ed.) (1984) *L. Krier: Houses, Palaces, Cities*, AD Profile 54 7/8.

Sherlock, H. (1991) *Cities Are Good for Us*, Paladin, London.

Tibbalds, F. (1992) *Making People-Friendly Towns*, Longman, London.

Trancik, R. (1986) *Finding Lost Space*, Van Nostrand Reinhold, New York.

Compact, Decentralised or What? The Sustainable City Debate

The deficiencies of today's post-industrial city reinforce the call for urgent action towards the improvement of the quality of life in the city and of its environmental impact in an ever-increasing number of publications, world conferences and research projects (particularly the WCED's Brundtland Report, 1987; the CEC's Green Paper, 1990; the UN's Earth Summit Agenda 21, 1993). Many of these reports contain sections which discuss the form and structure of a more sustainable city.

There are some who think that the city as we know it has no future, that in view of the development of ever more sophisticated communication systems there will, for many, soon be no need to work in the city centre or even in the city as is currently the case, and that the ability to work in and communicate from one's home will aggravate urban dispersal (Troy, 1996, p. 207). However, with an ever-growing majority of the globe's population living in conurbations we cannot simply abandon the city. It will continue to be the place where people work and live. Furthermore, the city is shaped by and expresses its history, the collective values and culture of its citizens which are important for their pride and the city's identity; it is a place into which vast efforts and huge sums of money have been invested which cannot simply be written off. The issue here is not the sustainable or unsustainable city; we cannot afford not to sustain the city. But it must become more readily and easily sustainable, economically as well as socially and environmentally. The all-important question is what form and structure would make the city more sustainable.

This chapter reviews the debate about the form and structure of a sustainable city. It investigates where the debate originated and compares the arguments for and against specific city forms and structures. It will become clear that the discussion is confused and inconclusive, not just because of its complexity but also because of the lack of precision in the description of urban models and a lack of focus of arguments. The call for more

inter-disciplinary and multi-aspect research is therefore not surprising; what is missing is tangible evidence and convincing empirical data that one or the other urban form is, or is more, sustainable.

Nevertheless, many demands for a more sustainable city or city region are shared by those involved in the debate, and ultimately a list of sustainability criteria emerges with the help of which the potential performance of city models can be compared and evaluated.

2.1 Starting Point of the Debate

The basis of the sustainable city debate is the general agreement that the city we know and inhabit today causes unsustainable environmental stress, is socially stratified and functionally suboptimal, and is expensive to run. The first important warning that changes are essential to safeguard resources for future generations was given by the Brundtland Report (WCED, 1987). It was soon followed by the *Green Paper on the Urban Environment* published by the European Commission in Brussels (CEC, 1990), which highlights functional, social, economic and environmental problems of today's cities and puts forward objectives and directives towards a more sustainable urban environment.

At the Rio Earth Summit it was agreed that 'indicators of sustainable development need to be developed to provide solid bases for decision-making at all levels and to contribute to self-regulating sustainability of integrated environmental and development systems' (United Nations, 1993). Both the EC Green Paper and Agenda 21 have considerable significance and impact on the debate about the city because of the political weight supporting them. In the UK, they were responded to at national level by a number of guidelines and directives, the most influential of which are:

- PPG13, published in March 1994 (DoE and DoT, 1994), which introduces a major change in policy by emphasising the interrelationship between land-use planning and transport, pointing out that the need to travel can be reduced by the appropriate location of development and by encouraging forms of development which promote sustainable modes of transport, including public transport. It also encourages the maintaining of existing urban densities and, where appropriate, an increase in density.

- PPG3: *Housing* (DoE, 1992), stressing the need to bring about a maximum amount of housing within urban areas and to reduce the need to travel.

- PPG6: *Town Centres and Retail Developments* (DoE, 1993), stressing the need to integrate retail outlets into, or adjacent to, urban cores.

- PPG15: *Planning and the Historic Environment* (DoE, 1994), which refers to 'the capacity of historic towns to sustain development'.

- The UK Strategy for Sustainable Development (UK Government, 1994) in response to the Rio Earth Summit. This highlights the role of the planning system and the need to derive policy that relates land uses and transport.

- PPG1 (revised): *General Policy and Principles* (DoE, 1997), which provides a more strategic view of the role of the planning system, specifically its contribution to achieving sustainable development. It summarises other policies (land use and transport; planning for housing; importance of the town centres; rural areas; conservation of historic environment), stresses the role of design considerations in planning and contains a new section on the Citizen's Charter and propriety.

All this indicates an awakening on the part of a wide section of professionals and politicians to the understanding that the city we have – with dense cores accommodating much of the city's workplaces, retail outlets, commerce, services and amenities; sprawling and low-density, single-use suburbs; a city structure which by default generates the need to travel and, owing to overall low population densities, car dependency and, as the result of the burning of fossil fuel, massive pollution; unattractive public transport because of low densities and underfunding; congested roads as a result of car dependency; and high energy consumption – is in the long term not sustainable owing to the destructive impact on the regional and global environment.

This understanding has generated a wide range of research projects and publications in search of sustainable urban development and living as a result of an improved form and structure for the city. Breheny's

statement is symptomatic: 'if cities can be designed and managed in such a way that resource use and pollution are reduced then a major contribution to the global problem can be achieved' (Breheny, 1992a, p. 2).

2.2 The Concept of the Compact City

The CEC Green Paper clearly calls for a return to the compact city, certainly influenced by the fact that many historic European towns and cities have densely developed cores which are seen as ideal places to live and work (mostly by those coming to visit these places for a short time, not necessarily by their inhabitants). Such places have high population densities which, the argument goes, encourage social mix and interaction which are the major characteristics of traditional cities. The UK government largely adopts the view of the European Commission, and this causes tensions with the English ideal of suburban living.

Arguments for the Compact City

The main supporters of the compact city – including the CEC (1990), Jacobs (1961), Newman and Kenworthy (1989), Elkin *et al.* (1991), Sherlock (1991), Enwicht (1992), McLaren (1992), Owens and Rickaby (1992) – believe that the compact city has environmental and energy advantages and social benefits (see Hillman, 1996, pp. 36–44; Thomas and Cousins, 1996, p. 56):

- a high degree of containment of urban development; reuse of infrastructure and of previously developed land; rejuvenation of existing urban areas and consequently urban vitality; as a result of containment and high population densities a compact city form and the conservation of the countryside;

- affordable public transport which meets the daily needs of those without a car, the majority of the urban population; as a result, increased overall accessibility and mobility;

- as a consequence of public transport reduced vehicular traffic volumes, related pollution and risk of death and injury in traffic; lower transport expenditure leading to less pollution; congestion spread over more roads and for shorter periods of time;

- viability of mixed uses as a result of overall high population densities; reduced travel distances as a result of mixed uses and overall higher population densities; cycling and walking as the most energy-efficient way of accessing local facilities; less car dependency;

- a better environment – due to overall reduced emissions and greenhouse gases and lower consumption of fossil fuel – and consequently better health;

- lower heating costs as a consequence of a denser urban fabric, with less energy consumption and less pollution;

- the potential of social mix as a result of high population densities, specifically when supported by a wide range of dwelling and tenure types in the neighbourhoods;

- concentration of local activities in communities and neighbourhoods; as a result a high-quality life, greater safety and a more vibrant environment as well as support for businessmen and services, i.e. a milieu for enhanced business and trading activities.

The main justification for the compact city is the need for the least energy-intensive patterns of activity to cope with the issues of global warming, concern about which was highlighted by the Inter-Governmental Panel on Climate Change (IPCC) in 1990, 1992 and 1995 (Hillman, 1996, p. 39).

Arguments Against the Compact City

There are many who insist that the case of the compact city is not proven,

> that there is evidence which suggests that these claims are at the least romantic and dangerous and do not reflect the hard reality of economic demands, environmental sustainability and social expectations. The overriding problem with the compact city is that it requires us to ignore the causes and effects of decentralisation, and benefits it may bring.
>
> (Thomas and Cousins, 1996, p. 56)

Or in other words, the compact city concept fails to acknowledge the poor prospects of reversing deep-seated decentralisation trends (Breheny, 1992a).

Some of the main arguments of those opposed to the compact city are:

- that the compact city concept contradicts the profound fondness for suburban and semi-rural living in the UK (Breheny, 1992a); that at particularly high densities the advantages of concentration might change into disadvantages through congestion which would outweigh energy consumption benefits of the compact city; that the fact that telecommunication allows people to live in the country contradicts the compact city concept (Breheny, 1992a);

- that the concept of the green city (also promoted by CEC (1990)) is in contradiction to that of the compact city (Breheny, 1992a); that open space

in cities would be taken up, that as a result the city's environmental quality would suffer;

- that the compact city policy would result in the neglect of rural communities and earlier growth centres which emerged under dispersal policy; that rural economic development would be threatened by a focus of activities within existing towns and cities (Breheny, 1992a);

- that the compact city would cause congestion, with the increased pollution, loss of amenity space and reduction of privacy so well demonstrated in cities like Calcutta, Cairo and Rio (Knights, 1996, p. 116);

- that in the compact city social segregation would grow as a result of the high cost of accommodation in the city centre and in the more privileged outer suburbs (van der Valk and Faludi, 1992, pp. 124–5);

- that the scale of energy savings through concentration may be trivial in comparison to the disbenefits it causes – e.g. in terms of unpopular restrictions on movement (Breheny, 1995);

- that optimum use of passive solar gain demands lower densities as the best energy savings are made with detached houses, semi-detached houses and bungalows; savings are less with terraced housing and less still with flats (NBA Tectonics, 1988; Breheny, 1992a);

- that the policy of a high-density, compact city fails to take account of the uncertainty in population growth and dispersal, i.e. that the compact city would not be able to respond to the predicted increase in the number of households (in the Netherlands half a million to one million new houses are said to be needed by 2015; in the UK over the next 20 years an extra 3.3 million single households are expected to require accommodation);

- that the power to affect local decisions and the viability of the provision of community facilities diminish with increasing scale of a compact city (McHarg, 1992, p. 153);

- that the compact city means massive financial incentives, which are economically suspect, and a high degree of social control, which is politically unacceptable (Green, 1996, p. 151).

The relationship between transport, urban form and energy consumption has been investigated in several research projects. Results are inconclusive. There is evidence that fuel consumption per capita is highest in more rural areas but there are indications that the largest cities (e.g. London) are likely to be less efficient than medium-sized and smaller towns, presumably as a result of congestion (Bannister, 1992, p. 165). Regarding urban density, intensity and energy consumption, higher-density cities tend to exhibit lower fuel consumption rates as a result of shorter travel distances and public transport; however, 'decentralised concentration', i.e. the promotion of urban and suburban cores, might be a fuel-efficient form (Bannister, 1992, pp. 171–4).

What Can be Learned from the Compact City Arguments and Counter-arguments

It is evident from this short review that research focusing on a single aspect – such as energy efficiency and transport or energy efficiency and urban form – is not likely to generate a reliable basis for the generation of concepts of a sustainable city or city region, and is not likely to come up with appropriate guidelines for planners, designers and politicians (see Breheny, 1992b). Energy issues, for instance, need to be balanced with social, economic and environmental objectives. Any improvement of one aspect of the city must be weighed against other benefits or losses.

What also needs to be taken into account is the fact that cities are all different in form and structure owing to a host of place-specific factors such as topography, history, climate, socio-economic conditions. It cannot be expected that they should all fit the same formula when it comes to the question of a sustainable city form. After all, we are generally confronted not with the task of planning and designing new towns and cities but, rather, that of replanning and redesigning existing cities, towns and settlements to make them more readily sustainable. The claim is made that the compact city is the most energy-efficient form of city, yet no investigation is made as to how much energy would be needed to change suburban sprawl into a compact city.

Furthermore, the question whether the transformation of an existing city into a compact city is economically and socially viable is largely ignored by those promoting that concept. Some cities may have the potential to become compact without substantial financial incentives; others may never become so unless massive financial support is made available, and, in view of the tendency to expect the private sector to take over responsibility for more and more of the city's infrastructure and public realm, it is highly unlikely that such support will be forthcoming. Other cities may have the potential to be partly compact and partly decentralised (as the case of Glasgow may prove).

But there are other arguments which also need to be taken into consideration and may well influence the choice of an overall viable urban form. The city of Edinburgh, for instance, already rather compact in parts, may well have the potential to become even more compact but in pursuit of this concept nobody, I hope,

would come up with the idea that Princess Street Gardens be developed, because that would destroy a unique city structure with old and new town in parallel, divided by the Gardens – quite apart from the fact that Edinburgh would lose one of its open linear spaces, the existence of which in close proximity to the highly dense old town may well render living there acceptable. By the same token, it is to be hoped that nobody would suggest, in pursuit of better environmental conditions, that a green wedge be driven through the city centre of Venice or Siena or Florence or any of the historic towns and cities with a highly dense core area.

What is suggested here is that the argument for or against a specific city form needs to take into account not only all the social, economic and environmental arguments and objectives but also the very specific structure and form of each individual city and its topographical, socio-economic and historical conditions. There may be a generally acceptable approach and there may be a shared set of objectives, but the implication of these will inevitably reflect the morphology of each individual settlement.

Then there is the problem that centrists focus their attention on the city and largely fail to discuss the relationship of the city with the countryside (with the exception of the compact city's reduced emissions as a consequence of reduced energy consumption). The city cannot exist on its own; it needs a hinterland to provide goods, food, raw materials, etc. The relationship of the city with its hinterland is therefore crucial. One point made by Susan Owens might have helped to provide additional focus for arguments, namely that the phrase 'urban sustainability' is a contradiction as 'cities will always be net consumers of resources drawing them from around the world. They are also likely to be major degraders of the environment, simply because of the relative intensity of economic and social activities in such places' (Owens, 1992, p. 79). It might therefore be more appropriate to search for structures and forms that result in a greater degree of sustainability for urban areas or regions, and investigate specifically the relationship between the city or conurbation and the countryside, rather than focus, as most of the centrists seem to do, on the sustainable city – and in this case the compact city only.

'Decentralised Concentration'

Many of those opposed to the compact city support the concept of 'decentralised concentration', the concept of a multi-nucleated city or even city region in which uses concentrated in the mono-core of the compact city are dispersed into a number of smaller centres forming the nuclei of urban districts or towns or 'villages'. The concept is based on the following policies on sustainable development and urban form (Breheny, 1992a, p. 22):

- Urban containment policies should continue to be adopted, and the decentralisation process slowed down.

- Compact city proposals, in any extreme form, are unrealistic and undesirable.

- Various forms of 'decentralised concentration', based around single cities or groups of towns, may be appropriate.

- Inner cities must be rejuvenated, thus reducing further losses of population and jobs.

- Public transport must be improved both between and within all towns.

- Mixed use must be encouraged in cities, and zoning discouraged.

- People-intensive activities must be developed around public transport nodes, along the Dutch 'right business in the right place' principle.

- Urban (or regional) greening must be promoted.

- Combined heat and power (CHP) systems must be promoted in new and existing developments.

It is clear that such changes cannot be achieved in a short period of time. 'The real challenge is ... to redesign existing urban form. Some important elements can be changed quickly (e.g. bus routes), other elements, such as railway and commercial buildings, can only be changed infrequently' (Breheny, 1992a, p. 22).

Compromise Positions

We have looked at the position of the 'centrists' and 'decentrists', but there is a group of 'compromisers', as regards their views on a sustainable urban form (Breheny, 1996, pp. 13–35; Scoffham and Vale, 1996, pp. 66–73; Thomas and Cousins, 1996, pp. 53–65). They advocate a combination of the merits of centralisation, i.e. urban containment and regeneration, with benefits of the 'inevitable decentralisation' to towns and suburbs (Breheny, 1996, p. 32). The 'compromisers' propose that individual neighbourhoods should involve the community and develop a strong identity and control over local resources (Scoffham and Vale, 1996, pp. 11–12).

Though not fully explained, the call for a degree of local autonomy is based on two convictions: that the people in a neighbourhood know best what their needs and aspirations are, and that they readily take more responsibility for and ownership of their neighbourhood if they have been involved in shaping it. The call for participation has considerable consequences for the city's form and structure. For communities to become successfully involved in the shaping of their own neighbourhoods requires decentralisation of power. This in turn necessitates the decentralisation of the city form and structure because a compact city or town, unless rather small, renders a participatory approach difficult if not impossible. The decomposition of the city or city region into smaller areas such as districts and neighbourhoods makes the communities' involvement feasible and effective but necessitates a framework at city region level for the integration of all development actions in districts and neighbourhoods. Decentralisation of the city is therefore a spatial, structural, functional, social and political phenomenon which expands into transport strategies and economics and requires also a certain degree of co-ordination at regional or even wider level to make the city and city region operate effectively.

To return to the arguments of the 'decentrists' and 'compromisers', they are reinforced by the fact that urban decentralisation – a process that started with the introduction of the railway and was exacerbated by the introduction of the car as a means of mass transport – is continuous, and is driven by powerful economic forces as well as the demand for what is considered to be a high quality of living by the middle- and upper-income groups. Centralised urban forms for them exemplify a way of urban living characteristic of the lower-income groups, those without the means to escape high-density housing (see Welbank, 1996, p. 78).

In the USA, Canada, Japan and Australia suburbanisation is massive. In Europe one can observe a process of counter-urbanisation, the suburbanisation of larger cities and towns, and the growth of smaller towns and villages (Breheny, 1996, p. 21). The UK government's containment policies such as the strategy for sustainable development (UK Government, 1994) and PPG13 on transport (DoE and DoT, 1994), based on the ECOTEC (1993) study, seem to be unable to stem this trend.

In view of this strong trend, and in view of the uncertainties of some of the qualities or perhaps deficiencies of the compact city – specifically with regard to the quality of environment provided and the quality of life in a dense environment – the old idea of the merger of the best of town and country reappears (Hooper, 1994; Lock, 1991, 1995), and so does the idea of Ebenezer Howard's concept of the 'Social City' in the form of a 'sustainable Social City' (Breheny and Rockwood, 1993).

Even the idea of social cohesion and equity as a result of high population densities in a compact city is questioned by the 'decentrists'. Welbank puts it this way:

our society is displaying all the characteristics of lack of social cohesion. We may not like this, we may feel it to be lamentable, but until such cohesion is re-established it is unlikely that forcing people into tight physical proximity will help at all – in fact, without the pre-existence of such cohesion it would actually be destructive. The enormous voluntary exodus from our cities demonstrates that the desire for social cohesion does not override the desire to live in suburbs and low density urbanised areas, given the benefits of mobility and technology.

(Welbank, 1996, p. 80)

There is a counter-argument to the claim that the compact city will be able to afford efficient public transport and will generate a socially more equitable community. Clean and uncongested public transport, so goes the argument, *allows* decentralisation because access to facilities relies on *speed* rather than *proximity* (Smyth, 1996, p. 107). If the model of the compact city is applied, the result will be a high concentration of workplaces and facilities in the compact city centre with resulting high land and property values which only high-income groups can afford. Middle-income groups will search for a place in the outer suburbs whereas the low-income groups will get stuck in a doughnut of social disadvantage, a transit zone surrounding the city centre. In essence, the compact city is socially exclusive (Smyth, 1996, p. 107). Such social stratification, according to this argument, can be avoided in a decentralised city with a series of compacted centres with smaller areas of lower-income groups located around them.

Confusion Regarding the Form and Structure of the Compact City

The concept of the compact city, as explained by the centrists, needs to be re-examined because it is still not clear what the structure and form of such a city might actually be. One's initial impression is that the compact city resembles the medieval city with the concentration of activities in a highly dense city with clear and abrupt edges to the countryside, usually in the form of a town wall (Thomas and Cousins, 1996, p. 54). But other descriptions do not seem to reinforce that impression.

'Centrist' Friends of the Earth suggest that a sustainable city 'must be of a form and scale appropriate to walking, cycling and efficient public transport, and with the compactness that encourages social interaction' (Elkin *et al.*, 1991, p. 12). This surely evokes the picture of a medieval city or perhaps Krier's '*quartiers*' (1984, pp. 70–1). But when Jenks *et al.* (1996), with reference to Haughton and Hunter (1994), summarise other suggestions of proponents of a sustainable city (p. 5) one may conclude that the compact city is not necessarily as compact and sharp-edged as the medieval city because the descriptions range from

- large concentrated centres, to

- decentralised but concentrated and compact settlements linked by public transport, to

- dispersal in self-sufficient communities (*Fig. 2.01*).

Though these suggestions are listed under the heading of 'The Compact City' it remains somewhat unclear

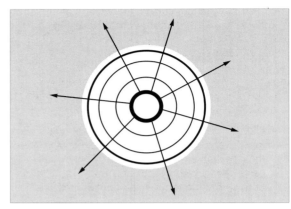

(a)

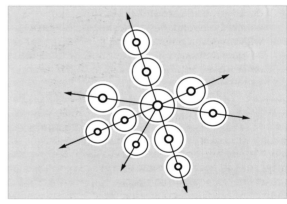

(b)

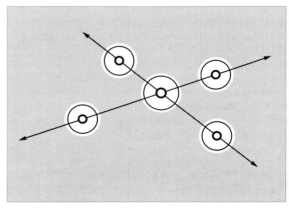

(c)

2–01. *Alternative forms of sustainable cities according to Haughton and Hunter (1994): (a) large concentrated centres; (b) decentralised but concentrated and compact settlements linked by public transport; (c) dispersal in self-sufficient communities* whether they refer to a compact city or alternative forms of sustainable city. The entire debate lacks clearer, more explicit descriptions of what the proponents see as the typical structure and form of a compact city, and this makes for confusion. Thomas and Cousins (1996, p. 54) also point to the lack of more explicit descriptions. They compare a number of descriptions of the properties of a compact city defined by different proponents:

- Elkin *et al.* (1991) list the following properties (pp. 16 and 43): intensification of use of space in the city; higher residential densities; centralisation; compactness; integration of land uses; and some form of self-containment.

- Newman and Kenworthy (1989) list the following characteristics: more intensive land use; centralised activity; and higher densities.

- Breheny and Rockwood (1993) demand high density; mixed use; and growth encouraged within the boundaries of existing urban areas with no development beyond the city's periphery (achieved through higher-density land use and reclamation of brownfield sites).

- Owens and Rickaby (1992) list two contrasting key patterns of settlements: centralisation and decentralised concentration.

In the last case it is clear that alternative forms of sustainable city are classified; in the other cases no clear image of a compact or sustainable city's form and structure emerge as both the compact city and the city based on the 'decentralised concentration' concept may have the properties listed, though compactness may refer to the city as an entity or to parts of the city.

It becomes somewhat clearer that there are several rather different views as to what a compact city is, that the compact city is not necessarily a homogeneous phenomenon (see Burton *et al.*, 1996, p. 235). A main difference of views seems to be whether the sustainable city should be monocentric or polycentric. Another difference seems to be with regard to the extent of homogeneous compactness on the one hand and the scale or overall dimension of a compact city on the other. Some seem to suggest that a sustainable city should be compact from core to edge, with large concentrated centres like the medieval city or town – in which case the overall dimensions of such a city may have to be relatively small if good access to open space outside the city for recreational and other purposes is to be achieved. Others seem to suggest that the city may consist of different compact settlements which are decentralised but linked by public transport, in which case the open space may be in between the settlements. The distance between such settlements may vary according to their degree of independence and self-sufficiency.

It seems that the argument for and against the compact city is unnecessarily complicated by the lack of definition of what kinds of concepts people have in their minds when discussing city form. It is therefore useful to highlight what all protagonists of different city models have in common; maybe the agreed properties of a sustainable city could form the basis for the generation of models of such a city. However, before I do so, another important dimension of a sustainable city, so far missing from this discussion, needs to be included: that of the ecology of the city and its relationship to the country.

The Ecological and Environmental Argument

The main argument of ecologists and environmentalists is that in order to achieve sustainable urban development and living it is not sufficient to solve problems of the wastage of energy and materials by behavioural changes and of pollution and congestion by introducing clean energy and promoting more energy-efficient public transport, or walking and cycling as alternative means of travel. The environmentalists argue that, in addition to all these important changes, the relationship of the city to the countryside has to change fundamentally. And this has considerable implications for the city's form and structure.

As the city is polluted and congested,

urban society now takes refuge in the countryside in search of fresh air and natural surroundings that are denied at home. Consequently, unsustainable pressures are placed on environmentally sensitive landscapes. The advancing city has often replaced complex natural environments of woods, streams and fields with biologically sterile man-made landscapes that are neither socially useful nor visually enriching.

(Hough, 1989, p. 2)

Hough argues further that in the city itself open spaces are not what they should be. The city, he states, incorporates vast areas of idle and unproductive land. Urban drainage, sewage disposal and other processes contribute to the pollution load. Parks are determined by horticultural science, not ecology. What is needed is the application of ecology to the process of designing a sustainable city. Traditional urban design, so the argument continues, has contributed little to the city's environmental health, nor has it created civilising, enriching places to live in. 'If urban design can be described as the art and science dedicated to enhancing the quality of life in cities, to provide civilising and enriching places for the people to live in them, then the current basis of urban form must be re-examined' (Hough, 1989, p. 12).

At the heart of this problem is the fact that the old symbiotic relationship between city and country no longer exists, that city and country have become mutually exclusive. Jane Jacobs has predicted that in the future the city will assume the role of supplier as well as consumer of resources (Jacobs, 1970). This can be achieved if what we throw away in form of waste materials, energy, garbage, waste water, vacant land, becomes a useful resource; if, as Girardet puts it, we change the linear metabolism (throwing away all the city's output) into a circular metabolism (in which all output of the city is recycled to become input) (Girardet, 1992, p. 22). This in turn means that the city has to become an eco-system in symbiosis with the countryside.

There is research evidence that open space distribution and forest vegetation cover influence urban climate, specifically when in the form of a finger plan with corridors of development and wedges of open space, as air-flow modelling in Chicago has concluded (Salvatore, 1982). Green wedges and woodland parks and natural forests in cities are, or can be if appropriately managed, more than green lungs or places for recreation (Hough, 1989, pp. 148–9):

- They allow interaction of urban and natural processes.

- They play a role in the maintenance of the water regime.

- They play a role in the modification of climate.

- They are outdoor laboratories for teaching forestation.

- They provide timber as alternative fuel, specifically when old trees need to be taken out.

Hough quotes Zürich as an example of a symbiotic relationship between the city and the countryside. With half a million people it is a city of similar size to Glasgow. Its park space covers nearly 25% of its urban area, and a major proportion of it is forest and common land, some 2,200 ha within a half-hour tram ride from the city centre. It provides timber for sawlogs and pulp; recreation and athletic facilities; wildlife; agriculture; visual amenity; education; and fitness tracks and exercise stops. Even deer are managed by the city authorities. In 1979 the cost of all recreation and forestry operations (including financial assistance to clubs) was SFr 4.5 million; the income from forest products was SFr 2.5 million, i.e. 55% of the total cost of the park system (Hough, 1989, p. 149). This not only demonstrates the environmental and social values of well-managed forests and common land but also that these can become economically productive for the city.

With natural and artificial corridors such as green wedges, streams and rivers, railway connections, canals, highways and transmission lines the city is connected to rural areas. These corridors greatly influence the migration and perpetuation of wildlife in cities. 'They maintain the links between natural habitats, parks, and open countryside' (Hough, 1989, p. 167).

Open land can also be successfully used for city farming. Girardet points out that

of China's 15 large cities, 14 have their own farm belts and are largely self-sufficient in food. The bulk of the food required by major cities . . . comes from their own agricultural suburbs, [where the soil] is kept fertile by treated human waste. Cities are intentionally compact, so as to leave as much room as possible for the farm belt. Only 20 and 40 percent of the land belonging to these cities is actually built on. The rural adjunct . . . which falls under the administration of the city, supplies most of the vegetables, grain, fruit, and meat required by the city's inhabitants. Industry is deliberately kept separate in other areas of the city.

(Girardet, 1992, p. 162)

Wade (1980) confirms that at least 85% of the vegetables consumed in China's cities are produced within the urban municipalities and that Shanghai and Peking are self-sufficient in vegetables, producing over 1 million tons per annum.

City farming, as a rural occupation in the city, was once common in our cities but is now largely a thing of the past because agriculture today is an industry, is large-scale and specialised, and with the growing size of the city, farming is too remote. But Hough (1989, p. 208) argues that 'with rising cost for food and energy, heightened environmental concern and increasing consciousness that fossil fuels cannot go on forever, there are signs that agricultural processes are changing'.

The fact that in a city like Glasgow there are waiting lists for allotments of up to three years indicates that the small-scale production of vegetables is very much a thing of the present. Riley (1979), from Friends of the Earth, confirms that the rising price of vegetables in the 1970s has resulted in an increase of home vegetable growing in the UK and that the waiting lists for allotments have grown by over 100,000 in less than 10 years.

Green wedges, the management of open linear spaces as eco-systems, city farming, small-scale food production in allotments – all this has design implications. Of vital importance are the city's open spaces, vacant land, derelict industry, contaminated land and brown sites as potential eco-systems and providers of resources. So here are strong arguments for the sustainable city to incorporate open space, forests and agricultural land. Rather than using it exclusively for new housing, some of the city's open space could be transformed into city farms and forests; and more land could be made available for such purposes if the built-up areas became more densely populated and if as a result the extent of the city's urban fabric actually shrank.

An open space strategy must therefore be part of the design framework for a sustainable city, just as much as compact neighbourhoods and districts with services and facilities in their cores; open space needs to be accessible by foot, bicycle and short public transport ride; it needs to be part of a sustainable city programme just as much as traffic-calmed streets within development clusters, neighbourhoods and districts, just as much as mixed use and public transport. A city must be sustainable not only functionally, economically and socially but also environmentally. None of these concerns can be left out in the search for a sustainable city form and structure.

Where Centrists, Decentrists and Compromisers and Others Agree

It is now possible to summarise all those characteristics which almost all of those involved in the debate believe a sustainable city should have. However, only those criteria and characteristics are included here that are generally valid and do not depend upon the existing morphological, climatic, topographical and socio-economic conditions and properties of a specific city, location or place.

Issues such as energy efficiency, cost of provision, cost of public transport, reduction of emissions and energy consumption, etc. are largely case specific and need to be referred to the study of actual cities or city regions. It is essential that research into a 'sustainable city model' be based on a balance of all the demands on, and properties of, the city and city region, and it is clear that focusing research on specific issues such as energy consumption or public transport is futile unless the findings are balanced with research into all other relevant issues. In this investigation I therefore decided to start with the general (all general aspects of city form and structure excluding those specific to particular cases and places) and move towards the specific (the investigation of an existing city region and its specific environmental, topographical, historical, socio-economic and other characteristics). This approach seems eminently sensible in the absence of any clear conclusion from recent research regarding almost all aspects of city form and structure.

But to return to the summing up of the debate, up to this point the account of what makes a sustainable city or city region has followed a somewhat erratic and in some cases rather disorganised sequence of arguments and counter-arguments. It is necessary to choose a more ordered approach for the comparison of city models. Therefore a parallel is drawn between Maslow's hierarchy of human needs, referred to in section 1.2, the demands on a city or city region that can be deduced from it, and the generally agreed sustainability criteria that resulted from the review of the sustainable city debate. There is no complete match but the sustainability criteria correspond roughly with Maslow's categories of needs. The comparison is documented in *Table 2.01*. In Chapter 3 the right-hand column of the matrix and its criteria will be applied in the same order for the evaluation of alternative city models.

There seems to be much more in common than an initial study of the arguments suggested. The differences seem to lie in the degree of compacting of the urban fabric and the degree of centralisation or decentralisation, rather than the principle. What is missing is some indication of these degrees. The decentrists put forward some models of a sustainable city applying decentralised concentration but only a general idea of the form and structure of a resulting city or city region emerges; the centrists do not sufficiently explain the structure and form of a compact city and, perhaps, much of the battle of arguments is caused by failure to provide this information.

There are some attempts to specify population densities in a compact city which range from sustainable urban net residential densities of between 225 and 300 persons per hectare (pph) (Friends of the Earth) to suggestions of optimal net residential densities of 90–120 pph to support public transport, and 300 pph to support services and facilities within walking distance (Newman & Kenworthy, 1989), but no evidence is made available as to how these figures have been derived. But there is another problem. Net densities may give a precise size of population for a limited area but do not provide a true picture of development density as they exclude other uses and all public space. High-density housing schemes, as for instance the high-rise dormitory towns of the 1960s and early 1970s in many of the UK's cities, concentrate a large number of people into a relatively small number of buildings, but these are frequently surrounded by so much open and generally unusable land that the overall population density is rather small; in such a case the net density figure may actually be misleading. Gross population densities – which indicate the population accommodated by the total area of a city or city region regardless of what the composition of uses and the size of all open space are – provide a much clearer picture of the development density of a town, city or conurbation and allow comparisons between different cities and city regions.

For these and other reasons the question of densities needs to be investigated in conjunction with the discussion of urban and residential models, without which the figures remain relatively meaningless. As Scoffham and Vale (1996, p. 66) point out, 'Density, in itself, is of little importance unless it is related to built form. Compact is meaningless unless it is related to some facts and figures.' Though this may be generally true, densities of population become rather important when they relate, regardless of the built form, to the viability of local services and facilities, public transport and energy efficiency. It may be true that, no matter how the city itself is structured, high-density housing is in the end socially acceptable to middle- and higher-income groups only if it provides the same quality of living as the country town would (and this necessitates the investigation of dense forms of family homes with garden or other forms of

Table 2–01. *Criteria for a more sustainable city form and structure compared with Maslow's hierarchy of human needs and the demands on the city that can be derived from it*

Maslow's hierarchy of human needs	What a 'good' city should provide	Commonly agreed sustainability criteria for the city and city region
1 Provision for all physical needs	• a place to live and work • a reasonable income • education and training • transport (mobility) and communication • access to services and facilities	Physical properties of the city/city region: • *some form of containment* of development to stem or even reverse sprawl and preserve the countryside; this can be aided through the reuse of underused and disused derelict and contaminated land to make it productive again, help make the city more compact and, by doing so to a tolerable degree, avoid unnecessary development of greenfield sites • *a reasonably high population density* to achieve viable local services and facilities, i.e. a high level of activities and interactions and thus vibrant settlement and places, and viable public transport • *a mixed-use environment*, specifically a higher concentration around public transport nodes in walking and cycling distance from people's front doors, in order to increase access to services and facilities and thus generate a vibrant environment, maybe even a sense of community, and to reduce to some degree the need to travel • *adaptability to changing socio-economic conditions* so that the city can change, expand and contract without major upheaval Provisions of the city/city region: • *public transport* in order to increase access to services and facilities, help reduce car dependency and thus congestion and pollution, achieve a reduction of energy consumption and help maintain a high level of energy-efficient and environment-friendly mobility inside the city or city region and between cities • *reduced traffic volumes and dispersed vehicular transport*, as a result of the availability of public transport and the design of road profiles, to avoid congestion of roads and urban areas • *a hierarchy of services and facilities* of different capacity and scale, from local provision in close proximity to one's front door to city centre provisions; this, together with a high degree of mobility, will increase choice • *access to green open spaces*, the city's green lungs, for recreation and sports, nature reserves, city farming, forestry, etc.
2 Safety, security and protection	• a visually and functionally ordered and controlled environment • a place free of pollution and noise • a place free of accidents and crime	Environmental and ecological conditions • *an environment free of pollution, noise, congestion, accidents and crime* • *personal private outdoor space* for each individual dwelling in form of gardens, roof gardens, terraces, loggias, etc. (without a return to low-density suburbs)

Maslow's hierarchy of human needs	What a 'good' city should provide	Commonly agreed sustainability criteria for the city and city region
		• *a symbiotic relationship of the city with the country* through the inclusion of open space linking directly with nature; the spaces to be used for forestation, farming, large-scale industries, sports and recreation, for the production of food and timber (for the construction industry, paper production and as renewable fuel) to make the city self-sufficient to as high a degree as possible
3 A conducive social environment	• a place where people have their roots and children their friends • a sense of community and belonging to a place or territory	Socio-economic conditions: • *social mix* to reduce or eliminate social and locational stratification, achievable through higher population densities and a wide range of dwelling and tenure types
4 A good image, reputation and prestige	• a place that provides a sense of confidence and strength • a place that gives a status and dignity • opportunity for individuals to shape their personal space	• *a degree of local autonomy*, the ability of individuals and the communities to shape their own environment according to their needs and aspirations; this would also support if not generate a sense of place and community, a sense of belonging • *a degree of self-sufficiency*, with different degrees of intensity, in terms of employment, energy (CHP), water, goods; the city not only as consumer but also as producer of goods
5 A chance to be creative	• opportunity for communities to shape their own districts and neighbourhoods	
6 An aesthetically pleasing environment	• a place that is well designed (aesthetically pleasing) • a place that is physically imageable • a city that is a place of culture and a work of art	Visual-formal quality • *imageability* of the city as entity and of the parts of the city, the neighbourhoods, districts and towns • *provision of a sense of centrality and place*

Note: CHP = combined heat and power

private outdoor space for inner-city areas) and if there is good access to an appropriate range of local services and facilities (see Green, 1996, p. 152). These services and facilities depend, however, upon a certain threshold value of population below which they cease to be economically viable. Such a threshold value of gross population density is therefore essential, though still somewhat elusive, and will have to be discussed later when city models are compared (see Chapter 3).

2.3 Conclusions
Up to this point in the discussion the exact forms and structures that – in conjunction with, or as a result of, all the properties listed above – would render the city more

sustainable remain elusive. It has become painfully evident that many of the claims in support of one or the other urban structure are not substantiated. There is no unimpaired evidence that one or the other city model would have a significantly higher or lower level of energy consumption, and investigations of the relationship between transport systems, densities and energy consumption are also largely inconclusive.

In view of the growing awareness of alternative sources of clean and renewable energy it seems only a matter of time until such sources become available on a viable economic scale. One has therefore to ask the question whether the search for a most energy-efficient city is in the long term not somewhat misguided. Reduction if not elimination of the use of fossil fuel for the generation of energy is essential not so much because this will preserve resources for future generations but because of the massive pollution that results from their use. For exactly this reason, future generations may actually not want to use these resources.

Sooner or later the quantity of energy consumed will become less relevant – on the one hand because it is clean, on the other because it is available in abundance. The major problem with car-dependent transport will then no longer be pollution but congestion, which is not solved by clean energy. Even with an abundance of clean energy, a form of urban transport is needed that uses less space; and this can be achieved by people sharing vehicles or vehicles forming trains or by efficient public transport systems. Accordingly, it is much more relevant to search for an urban form that responds to the sustainability criteria listed above, a city that is people-friendly, works efficiently and has a sustainable relationship with the regional and global hinterland. Further investigation concentrates therefore on the search for a structure that enables a high degree of mobility and access to a large variety of different services and facilities without causing congestion, a structure that allows a symbiotic relationship between city and country, a structure that enables social mix, a degree of autonomy of communities and a degree of self-sufficiency, and a structure that generates highly legible and imageable settlement forms. The following chapter will investigate models of the city that may partly or completely achieve the goal of bringing about a more sustainable city.

Needless to say, within the framework of this book it will not be possible to investigate exhaustively, and come up with empirical data for, the interdependence between demands for access to services and facilities by foot and their location; between population densities and viable local services and facilities; between public transport networks, access to them within walking distance, and population densities that render public transport viable. Such research will have to be carried out elsewhere, or is already being carried out. Nevertheless, these interdependencies will in principle be taken into consideration when studying alternative urban forms and structures. What it is hoped to achieve here is to bring about a clearer understanding of structures and forms of the city that *per se* achieve a considerable improvement in the city's quality and environmental impact even though the actual values of achievements are not yet accurately known and depend upon further, and case- and place-specific, research.

The investigation that follows focuses first and foremost on the city's micro-structure, which promises to support the case of a more sustainable city, and will then study alternative forms and macro-structures of the city and city region which provide some or all of the sustainability properties listed above.

References

Bannister, D. (1992) Energy use, transport and settlement patterns, in Breheny, M.J. (ed.) *Sustainable Development and Urban Form*, Pion, London.

Breheny, M.J. (1992a) Sustainable development and urban form: an introduction. In Breheny, M.J. (ed.) *Sustainable Development and Urban Form*, Pion, London.

Breheny, M.J. (ed.) (1992b) *Sustainable Development and Urban Form*, Pion, London.

Breheny, M.J. (1995) Compact city and transport energy consumption. *Transactions of the Institute of British Geographers*, NS, 20(1), pp. 81–101.

Breheny, M.J. (1996) Centrists, decentrists and compromisers, in Jenks, M., Burton, E. and Williams, K. (eds) *The Compact City: A Sustainable Urban Form?* E & FN Spon, London.

Breheny, M.J. and Rockwood, R. (1993) Planning the sustainable city region, in Blowers, A. (ed.) *Planning for a Sustainable Environment*, Earthscan, London.

Burton, E., Williams, K. and Jenks, M. (1996) The compact city and urban sustainability, in Jenks, M., Burton, E. and Williams, K. (eds) *The Compact City: A Sustainable Urban Form?* E & FN Spon, London.

Commission of the European Communities (1990) *Green Paper on the Urban Environment*, European Commission, Brussels.

Department of the Environment (1992) *Planning Policy Guidance 3: Housing*, HMSO, London.

Department of the Environment (1993) *Planning Policy Guidance 6: Town Centres and Retail Developments*, HMSO, London.

Department of the Environment (1994) *Planning Policy Guidance 15: Planning and the Historic Environment*, HMSO, London.

Department of the Environment (1997) *Planning Policy Guidance 1 (revised): General Policy and Principles*, HMSO, London.

Department of the Environment and Department of Transport (1994) *Planning Policy Guidance 13: Transport*, HMSO, London.

ECOTEC (1993) *Reducing Transport Emissions through Planning*, HMSO, London.

Elkin, T., McLaren, D. and Hillman, M. (1991) *Reviving the City: Towards Sustainable Urban Development*, Friends of the Earth, London.

Enwicht, D. (1992) *Towards an Eco-City: Calming the Traffic*, Envirobook, Sydney.

Girardet, H. (1992) *The Gaia Atlas of Cities: New Directions for Sustainable Urban Living*, Gaia Books, London.

Green, R. (1996) Not compact cities but sustainable regions, in Jenks, M., Burton, E. and Williams, K. (eds) *The Compact City: A Sustainable Urban Form?* E & FN Spon, London.

Haughton, G. and Hunter, C. (1994) *Sustainable Cities,* Jessica Kingsley Publishers, London.

Hillman, M. (1996) In favour of the compact city, in Jenks, M., Burton, E. and Williams, K. (eds) *The Compact City: A Sustainable Urban Form?* E & FN Spon, London.

Hooper, A. (1994) Land availability and the suburban option. *Town and Country Planning,* 63(9), pp. 239–42.

Hough, M. (1989) *City Form and Natural Process,* Routledge, London and New York.

Jacobs, J. (1961) *The Death and Life of Great American Cities,* Vintage Books/Random House, New York.

Jacobs, J. (1970) *The Economy of Cities,* Vintage Books/ Random House, New York.

Jenks, M., Burton, E. and Williams, K. (eds) (1996) *The Compact City: A Sustainable Urban Form?* E & FN Spon, London.

Knights, C. (1996) Economic and social issues, in Jenks, M., Burton, E. and Williams, K. (eds) *The Compact City: A Sustainable Urban Form?* E & FN Spon, London.

Krier, L. (1984) Houses, palaces, cities, in Papadakis, A. (ed.) *Architectural Design* Profile 54.

Lock, D. (1991) Still nothing gained by overcrowding. *Town and Country Planning,* 60(11/12), pp. 337–9.

Lock, D. (1995) Room for more within city limits? *Town and Country Planning,* 64(7), pp. 173–6.

McHarg, I.L. (1992) *Design with Nature,* John Wiley & Sons, New York.

McLaren, D. (1992) Compact or dispersed? Dilution is no solution. *Built Environment,* 18(4), pp. 268–84.

NBA Tectonics (1988) *A Study of Passive Solar Energy Estate Layout,* Department of Energy, London.

Newman, P.W.G. and Kenworthy, J.R. (1989) *Cities and Automobile Dependency: An International Source Book,* Gower Technical, Aldershot.

Owens, S. (1992) Energy, environmental sustainability and land-use planning, in Breheny, M.J. (ed.) *Sustainable Development and Urban Form,* Pion, London.

Owens, S. and Rickaby, P.A. (1992) Settlements and energy revisited, in Breheny, M.J. (ed.) The compact city, *Built Environment,* 18(4), pp. 247–52.

Riley, P. (1979) *Economic Growth, the Allotments Campaign Guide,* Friends of the Earth, London.

Salvatore, F. (1982) *The Potential Role of Vegetation in Improving the Urban Air Quality: A Study of Preventative Medicine,* York–Toronto Lung Association, Willowdale, Ontario.

Scoffham, E. and Vale, B. (1996) How compact is sustainable – how sustainable is compact?, in Jenks, M., Burton, E. and Williams, K. (eds) *The Compact City: A Sustainable Urban Form?* E & FN Spon, London.

Sherlock, H. (1991) *Cities Are Good for Us,* Paladin, London.

Smyth, H. (1996) Running the gauntlet, in Jenks, M., Burton, E. and Williams, K. (eds) *The Compact City: A Sustainable Urban Form?* E & FN Spon, London.

Thomas, L. and Cousins, W. (1996) The compact city: a successful, desirable and achievable urban form?, in Jenks, M., Burton, E. and Williams, K. (eds) *The Compact City: A Sustainable Urban Form?* E & FN Spon, London.

Troy, P.N. (1996) Environmental stress and urban policy, in Jenks, M., Burton, E. and Williams, K. (eds) *The Compact City: A Sustainable Urban Form?,* E & FN Spon, London.

UK Government (1994) *Sustainable Development: The UK Strategy,* HMSO, London.

United Nations (1993) *Earth Summit Agenda 21: The UN Programme of Action from Rio,* United Nations, New York.

van der Valk, A. and Faludi, A. (1992) Growth regions and the future of Dutch planning doctrine, in Breheny, M.J. (ed.) *Sustainable Development and Urban Form,* Pion, London.

Wade, I. (1980) *Urban Self-Reliance in the Third World: Developing Strategies for Food and Fuel Production,* World Future Conference, Toronto.

Welbank, M. (1996) The search for a sustainable urban form, in Jenks, M., Burton, E. and Williams, K. (eds) *The Compact City: A Sustainable Urban Form?* E & FN Spon, London.

World Commission on Environment and Development (1987) *Our Common Future,* Oxford University Press, Oxford.

Micro- and Macro-structures of a More Sustainable City

3

The debate on a sustainable city form has so far been rather disappointing and has not produced much over and above the list of generally accepted sustainability criteria. Confused definitions and research focusing on a limited number of aspects (such as efficiency in terms of energy, transport, etc.) have not generated reliable answers to the question of a more sustainable city form in terms of energy efficiency, viability of public transport and of services and facilities. Research results are inconclusive and no clear city model emerges that promises to be definitely preferable to other models.

It therefore seems appropriate to start research at the other end of the list of properties of a city; that is, to look for those models that promise a high degree of user-friendliness. Once city models have been established that respond positively to the relevant sustainability criteria listed at the end of the previous chapter the investigation will be able to focus more effectively on issues such as energy efficiency, reduction of pollution, economic viability, etc. This reversed approach, in comparison with much current research, eliminates unsuitable models in social and functional terms and accordingly limits the range of models to be further investigated.

This chapter therefore focuses on the more detailed analysis of alternative city forms. The first investigation concentrates on the impact of the criteria of sustainability on the micro-structure of the city or city region. Of specific interest will be the impact of demands for access to public transport and to local services and facilities by walking and cycling for the pattern of development clusters and provision centres. These demands are valid for any kind of city; the resulting micro-structure – a hierarchy of provision nodes and linkages of different capacity – can accordingly be expected to be applicable regardless of what the macro-structure of a city may be.

Then alternative macro-structure models are studied which illustrate different configurations and develop-ment patterns of the city region or metropolis. The objective of this investigation is to find out how the individual models compare in terms of overall dimensions and the total area required and how they respond to the sustainability criteria of Chapter 2. In order to make the city models truly comparable, certain conditions are imposed: the same average gross population density, the same total population, and the inclusion of the same amount of open land in the city area apply for all models. The resulting overall dimensions and total areas for each of the models are then compared and reveal little overall difference at smaller total population; differences emerge only with one model at larger total population. This clearly indicates that, under given conditions, the actual form of the models has relatively little influence on the required area, though travel distances differ somewhat. However, evaluation of the potential performance of the individual city models on the basis of the sustainability criteria clearly indicates the advantages and disadvantages of each model depending upon the weight given to individual criteria. But when the degree of restructuring of existing cities and conurbations as a result of the application of the models is reflected upon and the suitability of the models for efficient transport structures is taken into consideration, it becomes clear that city models with a more rigid geometry are less suitable and the polycentric net with its random geometry and transport grid more suitable for application.

The chapter concludes that the investigation has produced a generally valid micro-structure and has strengthened the argument for a composite city form. Another conclusion is that there is no single sustainable city form; the choice of a planning and design approach for the improvement of an existing city or city region depends entirely upon the characteristics of that city or city region and may therefore have to be different in each case.

3.1 The Micro-structure of a More Sustainable City

Comparisons of city forms and structures must be based on a reasonably accurate understanding of the micro-structure behind such forms, without which no definite answers regarding the achievements of this city model are possible. What now need to be studied are the constituent parts of the city and their role within a specific city form, their relationship to transport networks and to the location of nodes, of centres of provision.

Fundamental Demands on the City Structure

Three major demands are made on the city and its districts which need to be reflected in the micro-structure of the city: accessibility, proximity and functional mix (see Ciuffini, 1995, p. viii). Regarding access to services and facilities, it is generally agreed that public transport has to play an essential role in order to reduce congestion and pollution. Research has shown that it is also the most economic way to facilitate mobility in the city (Ciuffini, 1995, pp. xvi, 32–4). Public transport depends on a certain population density, and, perhaps even more importantly in this context, upon ease of access. Public transport stops should accordingly be provided within walking distance of housing and workplaces. This in turn necessitates a modular city structure, a city composed of small urban 'cells', or 'proximity units' (Ciuffini, 1995, pp. xix and 29–40), which have pedestrian scale and provide good access to public transport stops within walking distance. If local amenities are located at the transport node, then they are equally well accessed by the communities of these 'cells'. The 'cells' themselves need to be linked with each other by public transport lines to provide choice of amenities and mobility.

The interrelationship of people, transport and amenities is thus the basis for the micro-structure of the city. However, a distinction has to be made between 'cells' of different size and population. Because those urban 'cells' which provide local services and facilities within walking distance are inevitably small not only in size but also in population; they cannot therefore afford to provide for anything other than day-to-day needs. Provision beyond that scale has to be catered for by centres of a higher order at the heart of larger spatial units, for instance urban districts, formed by clusters of small urban 'cells'. These are linked with each other by a public transport system of higher order, for instance light rail transit (LRT). Districts in turn may form clusters around a centre of provision of yet higher order, for instance town centres linked with each other by a transport system of yet higher order, for instance the railway; and so on. In short, the micro-structure of the city is expected to be hierarchical with regard to both the development of clusters (from neighbourhood to districts, town, city, each with appropriate centres of provision) and the

transport systems (from bus to LRT to railway with appropriate nodes of transport intersections at the centres of the respective spatial units). This structure and the nature of the different spatial units need to be investigated in more detail.

The Urban Neighbourhood

Almost all publications concerned with access to public transport agree that the maximum distance between one's front door and a transport stop is the length of a path one can walk in 10 minutes. Interpretations as to what this means in metres differ somewhat, but about 600 m distance between the edge of a neighbourhood and its central area and transport node seems to be a generally accepted measure. The catchment area accordingly has a size of about 110–120 ha of built-up area (to which a certain amount of open land may be added). With an average gross population density of say 60 persons per hectare (pph), such an area would accommodate about 7,000 persons (Fig. 3.01).

The choice of a gross population density is important as it needs to be sufficiently high to generate, in the limited area of a neighbourhood defined by walking distances (i.e. with a radius of 600 m), a population large enough to support local services and facilities which provide for daily needs. (It is important this population should be mixed, as regards income levels.) The viability of a density figure will be reviewed in section 3.3 in a discussion of the conditions for the comparability of city models and will be scrutinised in case studies in Chapters 5 and 6.

Area and distance between edge and centre are fairly similar to that of a neighbourhood of new towns in the UK, frequently 1 km^2, and almost identical in size and population with Calthorpe's urban transit-oriented developments (TODs; Calthorpe, 1993, p. 57). Services and facilities would best be located at the centre of the neighbourhood and around the transport

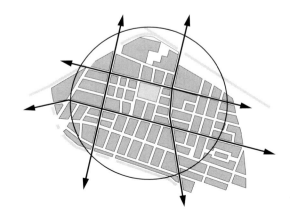

3–01. Urban neighbourhood: Govanhill, Glasgow

node, thus contributing to the creation of a meaningful central place. The neighbourhood is therefore the smallest 'building block' or 'unit' of which the city is made up.

There are many who do not believe in the viability of a neighbourhood structure, for several reasons. There is an argument that people who live in a neighbourhood may not necessarily use the local services and facilities but those in other areas of the city, either as a matter of preference or because they are located close to their workplace or on the way to or back from school, or for a variety of other reasons. Christopher Alexander, by quoting Ruth Glass's redevelopment plan for Middlesbrough, makes it quite clear that the physical units defined by the city's various social systems do not all define the same neighbourhood. Catchment areas for schools, youth clubs, adult clubs, post offices and grocers are not limited to the neighbourhood in which they are located but overlap with other neighbourhoods (Alexander, 1988, pp. 76–7). According to Alexander, building up a city from neighbourhood units therefore generates a rigid structure which does not coincide with the social systems in an open society. Therefore such a structure is unacceptable.

The argument, which refers to new and specifically to zoned town and city development during the 1960s, is somewhat at odds with the structure of traditional towns, which in the same article are appreciated as examples of complex urban models with a lattice rather than a tree structure, as places that allow spontaneous interaction of people with people and with elements of the physical urban systems. The principle of what Bacon calls 'dominant and subdominant centres' in traditional cities like, for instance, Venice and Florence clearly indicates that towns were hierarchically structured (Bacon, 1992, p. 101). The medieval merchant city of Venice shows a very clear structure of neighbourhoods defined and physically separated by canals *(Fig. 3.02).*

Each neighbourhood, the territory of a guild and therefore with a concentration of specific uses, would have a central place, a subdominant centre, with church and fountain, guild-hall and school; St Mark's would be the dominant centre. Though rigorously zoned, the overall structure was that of a nuclear but open plan which, according to Mumford, 'would, if imitated, have overcome the tendency to provide for extension by solid massing and overcrowding and sprawling, in the fashion of other expanding cities' (Mumford, 1984, pp. 370–1). The neighbourhood structure of Venice developed and expanded from, originally, six islands for six guilds by the creation of other islands for other guilds and for industry. Howard's idea of city growth by multiplication of units rather than extension obviously had a precedent. Renaissance Florence shows a similar structure of dominant and subdominant centres, though the neighbourhoods do not have clear physical boundaries and may actually have overlapped *(Fig. 3.03).*

A strict limitation of people to a specific area in a city and to specific local provisions as in the merchant city of Venice is today unthinkable; the lack of social cohesion in our society has already been referred to. What is called *neighbourhood* in this context does not, therefore, equate with a social group but a group of independent people sharing access to certain amenities located in walking distance from their home, whether they use these amenities or those provided elsewhere. Following Christaller's central place theory, in physical terms the city structure may well be hierarchical, from neighbourhood to district to city in terms of catchment areas for services and facilities of different calibre (Christaller, 1933) *(Fig. 3.04).* However, this structure in no way prevents people from having a free choice as to which of these areas they frequent and which of their services and facilities they use – provided they are mobile; hence the importance of mobility in the city or city region.

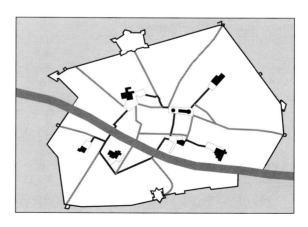

3–02. Neighbourhood structure of medieval Venice *(diagrammatic plan based on a historical map and Bacon, 1992, pp. 102–3)*

3–03. Neighbourhood structure of Renaissance Florence *(diagrammatic plan based on a historical map and Bacon, 1992, p. 106)*

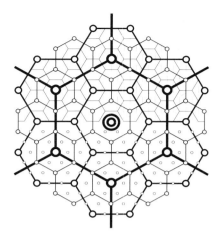

3–04. *Centres of provisions for different catchment areas (diagram after Christaller, 1933)*

The most important argument for a neighbourhood structure and neighbourhood centres is that they provide services and facilities for those less mobile, especially the elderly, young mothers with small children, the disabled. For these people access within walking distance to local services and facilities is vital, and equally so access to public transport, which allows them to benefit from other and larger-capacity provision centres elsewhere in the city or city region.

There is an argument that questions the economic viability of neighbourhood centres of provision. Because of the limited population accommodated in a neighbourhood and the fact that many of those who are sufficiently mobile satisfy their needs elsewhere in the city rather than in their own area, neighbourhood centres provide only the most basic services and facili-

ties, provide little choice and are expensive. The fact that many corner shops have closed seems to be a clear indication of the economic difficulties facing neighbourhood provision *(Fig. 3.05)*. The problems such facilities face have to do with the economy of scale. Retail outlets, for instance, are getting bigger and bigger and are locating in out-of-town places or outside urban districts, where they find plenty of inexpensive land. Small shops cannot compete with provisions in such retail parks, offer a much reduced range of goods, need to be kept open for long hours for their owner to make a living, and therefore find it difficult to remain viable.

However, retail parks, now also accommodating restaurants and entertainment and other facilities that make shopping a 'day out' event, depend almost entirely on access by car and discriminate against those who cannot afford a car or are not mobile for other reasons. With growing awareness of congestion as a consequence of car dependency, trends towards walking and cycling and the use of public transport should help local facilities and services to become more viable because more people will depend on them. As discussed in Chapter 2, governmental policies, specifically PPG13 on transport (DoE and DoT, 1994) and PPG6 on town centre and retail development (DoE, 1993), indicate a clear trend towards the support of local provisions and of public transport. But guidelines alone will not sufficiently reduce the use of the car. Other restrictive measures – such as, for instance, road pricing, a substantial increase in petrol tax, reduction of parking places in built-up areas – will be required to convince people that walking, cycling and the use of public transport are preferable to the use of the car (see Williams *et al.*, 1996, pp. 91–4; Moughtin, 1996, pp. 50–1). The precondition is, of course, the availability of effective, co-

3–05. *Neighbourhood shops at Clevenden Road, Kelvindale, Glasgow*

ordinated, fast, comfortable and inexpensive public transport systems.

If, as a result of such measures and the introduction of public transport systems, the use of the car becomes more and more restricted, at least in central areas of urban 'cells', as seems to be eventually inevitable, then the neighbourhood centre may become more readily supported by people in its vicinity, which in turn may generate better-quality services and facilities.

There are clear signs of the renewed appreciation of the neighbourhood as a viable city building unit. During the past few years mini-supermarkets have been opening in neighbourhood positions, provided by companies that seem to have detected a gap at the bottom end of the hierarchy of retail provisions *(Fig. 3.06)*. Breheny suggests that the creation or re-creation of small, intimate neighbourhoods is part of a renewed interest in community-level solutions, and he points to new urban villages in the UK (Urban Villages Group, 1992) and the 'new-traditionalist' developments in the USA, the small community of Seaside in Florida (Duany and Plater-Zyberk, 1991) and Calthorpe's TODs (Calthorpe, 1993) as examples (Breheny, 1996, pp. 28–9). Another example is the design proposal for Avalon Park in Orlando, Florida, with four areas of a 5 minute walk radius forming a neighbourhood (see Koetter, 1992, p. 18). Urban neighbourhoods, linked by a public transport system, form the structural units of Seattle's approach to the replanning of the city (see Lawrence, 1996, pp. 23–5). Scoffham and Vale (1996, p. 72) call for the re-examination of proposals for structuring neighbourhoods, and suggest that a radius of 600 m is reasonable and that within this radius local autonomy can be encouraged.

As non-work-related trips to shops, schools, recrea-tional facilities and the like represent about 70% of all trips, efficient public transport providing access to district and city centres on the one hand and local provision accessed by foot and bicycle on the other could contribute to a potentially significant reduction of the use of the car with all its consequences in terms of the reduction of congestion and pollution. (See Farthing *et al.*, 1996, pp. 185–8.) But even if the contribution of local centres to the reduction of trips overall might be relatively small, the neighbourhood units, owing to their small size and population, enable effective participation by the community in the shaping of its area; that is they enhance local autonomy. Furthermore, the neighbourhood centres can provide a sense of place and focal point. For all these reasons the neighbourhood needs to be recognised as an essential building unit of the city.

Regarding the provisions in the neighbourhood, there should be a variety of house types, from flats in high-density low-rise housing to terraces and other forms of family homes; mixed dwelling and tenure types will encourage a mixture of social and income levels in the neighbourhood, which in turn will help secure the viability of services and community provisions. Densities may vary between the central area and the edge of the neighbourhood as suggested for Calthorpe's TODs (Calthorpe, 1993, p. 59), but mixed forms of housing provision, e.g. tenement or terrace with mews cottages along lanes as typical for Glasgow *(Fig. 3.07)*, may also achieve continuous densities, i.e. similar conditions at centre and edge without loss of housing mix. The example shows that on 1 ha of land with three-storey tenements a density of 190 persons per hectare is achieved (land including 50% of surrounding streets and car parking, lane and gardens). With four-storey tenements the density would rise to over 245 persons per

3–06. *Neighbourhood shops at Dorchester Avenue, Kelvindale, Glasgow*

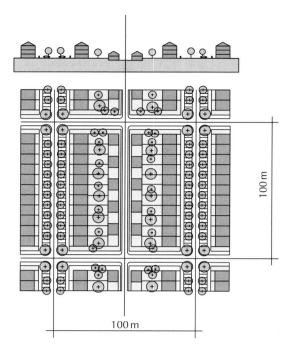

100 m

100 m

3–07. *Density of urban block with a mixture of housing provision*

hectare without generating unpleasant environmental conditions.

The neighbourhood should provide a mixed-use centre with public transport stop, housing over shops and service outlets, with a market place and community park with community hall, a number of shops for daily needs and a small supermarket, a post office counter, a public house, a newsagent, a local bank and library, local (medical and dental) surgeries, commercial units and other workplaces. The neighbourhood should also accommodate a number of kindergartens, a primary school and youth facilities, play and sports areas for children and youngsters, and allotments. The neighbourhood core may have an area of about 1 ha.

Traffic in the neighbourhoods should be calmed, and through traffic kept outside completely. Car-parking places should be confined to serving the local population, so as to encourage the use of public transport for all those travelling into the neighbourhood from outside. The neighbourhood centre specifically should not provide any car parking at all – except for vehicles of disabled people and perhaps for taxis – to discourage the use of the car as a means to travel to central facilities.

Clusters of Neighbourhoods Forming Urban Districts

With the support of restrictive measures to limit the use of the car within urban areas, the neighbourhood provi-

sion centre might become economically more viable and socially more acceptable. But with its limited services and facilities, it cannot provide for more than basic day-to-day needs and cannot supply goods and services beyond the capacity of the neighbourhood community. Other centres of higher capacity are therefore needed which serve larger catchment areas. If the next larger centre is the city centre itself, as in the UK's new towns or as in Calthorpe's TODs, then all services and facilities other than those accommodated in neighbourhoods would be concentrated in the city's core area and this would result in the need for everyone to travel to the centre for all goods and provisions other than those for daily needs. This in turn would result in congested transport lines in the more central areas of the city. Though there may well be a historical city centre with a concentration of specialist retail and entertainment facilities and most likely also with a kind of central business district, facilities the city centre does not necessarily depend upon should therefore be decentralised into district centres.

If several neighbourhoods, say four or five of them, were to form a district, its core might become the focus for a much larger population of 25,000–35,000; that is the district would have the size and population of a small to medium-sized country town *(Fig. 3.08)*. The district core would be linked with the neighbourhood centres by public transport, say buses with stops every 300 m or so. Travel distances would be in the region of 1,300–1,450 m and travel from the edge to the centre of the district would take about 5 minutes; the core area may have a radius of 150 m and an area of about 7 ha. The plan for the structuring of Seattle already mentioned suggests such a structure: in denser areas of the city, clusters of neighbourhoods make up a 'regional urban centre' which would be accessible from neighbourhoods with the help of small coaches and vans; express buses would link the regional system to the central business district (Lawrence, 1996, p. 25).

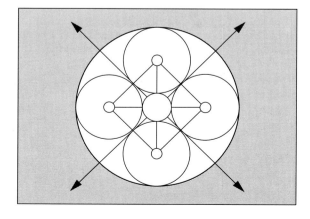

3–08. *The urban district as agglomeration of neighbourhoods*

Such districts would have a sufficiently large catchment area to accommodate commerce and other workplaces, a retail core with a large supermarket, a do-it-yourself shop, some specialist shops, restaurants, banks, a post office, cultural facilities, public houses, a cinema, entertainment and sports facilities including an indoor swimming pool, a secondary school, a district hospital. The district centres would be linked by faster transport to other district centres and the city centre, for instance in the form of LRT. They would be highly imageable and full of vitality, particularly if each of them had different design characteristics and perhaps also a different dominant use (as, for instance, urban districts in the city centre of Paris have). Again a central market and park area would help to create a focus. The district could be semi-autonomous, with its own 'district hall' in which representatives of the neighbourhood communities would meet to take decisions concerning the development and shape of their area. Clearly, in all its characteristics an urban district should resemble an independent market town, with the difference that the district is part of a system of closely linked and related areas within a city net.

Vehicular traffic cannot be kept out of consideration, not only because of the need for access by service and emergency vehicles but because people will not want to give up their prerogative of owning and also driving a car. There are two principal solutions for dealing with vehicular traffic in districts:

- to keep vehicles outside the district (as in the UK new town neighbourhoods) with culs-de-sac leading into the neighbourhoods; this generates a car-free central district area which accommodates only public transport, cycles and pedestrians *(Fig. 3.09a)*;

- to allow vehicular traffic to share road space with public transport, cycles and pedestrians but calm vehicular traffic and give priority to all other forms of transport *(Fig. 3.09b)*.

Separating traffic generates problems of the perception of the path system and of permeability and ease of access and cannot, therefore, be the preferred option. Pure pedestrian streets are meaningful and necessary really only if large numbers of people frequent a particular space; restriction of vehicular transport in all other streets is not necessary as they can be designed in such a way that all types of transport may share zones of the same space. However, only local vehicular transport should be allowed inside the district, sharing road space with buses and LRT but with public transport clearly having priority, as for instance in Zürich, as seen in 'California Dreaming', a BBC2 *Horizon* programme shown in 1991.

Roads inside districts can be zoned such that access to public transport from pavements is direct; this would

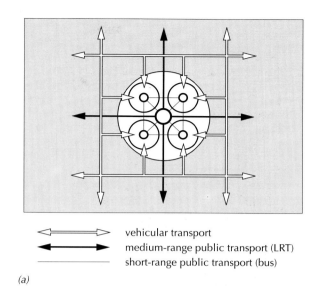

vehicular transport
medium-range public transport (LRT)
short-range public transport (bus)

(a)

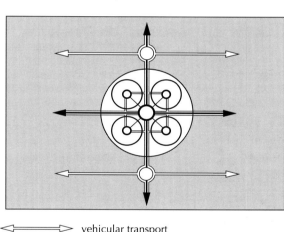

vehicular transport

medium-range public transport

local vehicular transport and short-range public transport

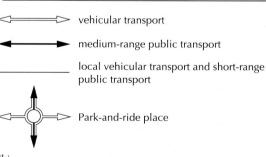

Park-and-ride place

(b)

3–09. The relationship between public and private transport in districts. (a) Vehicular and public transport spatially separated; (b) Vehicular and public transport sharing road space

result in public transport being located at the edges of the road towards the pavements, other vehicular transport to use the central lanes. At crossing points vehicular traffic should be calmed and buses or LRT should get automatic green lights whenever they are approaching a street crossing. Only major vehicular transport routes such as expressways and motorways for inter-city traffic should be outside and between districts; they should be sunken to prevent them from becoming barriers, and should be intensely greened and landscaped to reduce pollution and noise and to operate as one of the linear artificial green spaces that may attract wildlife and help improve the city's climate. At junctions of such expressways and motorways with public transport routes park-and-ride places should be established to allow easy interchange from vehicular inter-city traffic to public transport within the city and its districts.

Clusters of Districts Forming Larger Towns

District centres would still provide for a limited number of people. Therefore centres of a yet higher order could be generated at the heart of say four to five urban districts, serving a larger population of between 120,000 and 175,000 *(Fig. 3.10)*. In many cities the process of decentralisation has already generated such centres but many of them, as Glasgow will demonstrate later, are out-of-town places of no urban quality. They need to be transformed into proper town centres with mixed uses, including housing. Such centres, with a radius of about 300 m and an area of 28 ha, may provide economically viable specialist services and facilities. In addition to retail outlets and commerce, town centres and towns may include outdoor and indoor sports facilities, swimming baths, conference centres, hotels, entertainment centres, theatres and concert facilities, central hospitals, colleges and universities. There should also be a town hall and local administration centre, staffed by representatives of the districts forming the town, and responsible for the town's development and structure. Access to town centres may be provided by LRT; travel distances from edge to core may be between 2,900 and 3,200 m and travel time not more than 10 minutes.

A Cluster of Towns Forming a City

In larger conurbations a number of say four or five towns may form a city with a population of between 480,000 and 875,000 with a city centre, usually the historical core of the conurbation *(Fig. 3.11)*. The central area, with a minimum radius of about 600 m and an area of 110–120 ha, may have a similar profile of uses to those of town centres but may include a high proportion of housing to make the centre an inhabited mixed-use area. It may also accommodate specific city centre uses: a major regional administration centre, perhaps also a concentration of cultural and entertainment facilities. Transport linkages between town centres and between these and the city centre would be by LRT. Maximum distances between edges of the towns and the city centre may be 6,400–7,000 m and travel time by LRT should not exceed 20 minutes. Railway lines would link the city centre to other cities, airports and sea ports and to other parts of the country. In contrast to the mono-core city this hierarchical structure is achieved through the decentralisation of functions and activities, which in turn may achieve a degree of decentralisation of transport. In a sense this city structure resembles a compacted satellite city but the satellites are not separated from the central city by open country.

The Composite Structure of the City or City Region

Following the model of such a micro-structure, the city or city region is an agglomeration of linked towns which themselves are an agglomeration of linked districts each of which is an agglomeration of linked neighbourhoods. Towns, districts and neighbourhoods each have their own identity and their own centre which in scale of services and facilities responds to the scale of the urban areas it serves. Parallel to this hierarchical composition of spatial and formal entities is the provision of a hier-

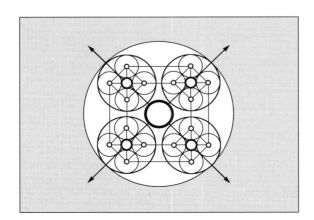

3–10. The town as agglomeration of districts

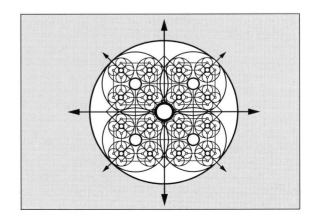

3–11. The city as agglomeration of towns

archical system of public transport from railway to LRT and bus and of private transport from primary to district and local distributors (with the LRT and bus network on district and local distributors). This system provides access to places in the city, districts and neighbourhoods, operating as a linked system with intersections and junctions and allowing easy interchange from one transport network to the others. Mobility within such a linked system is high, and travel by public transport is comfortable, especially if transport nodes are well-designed, sheltered places, integrated into centres of services and facilities. Furthermore, railway, LRT and buses feed passengers to one another rather than competing for passengers over the entire city network. This system also enables uses to locate at the most suitable places with the appropriate access by rail, LRT and bus, by motorway, district and local distributors, or by a combination of public and private transport (compare the A, B and C locations and their accessibility profile in the Netherlands; Ministry of Housing, Physical Planning and the Environment, 1991, pp. 15–17).

The structure as well as the image of such a net city is provided by the different nodes and areas, the towns, districts and neighbourhoods and their mixed-use central areas, and by the linkages between them, very much as suggested by Lynch in his proposals to structure the metropolis (Lynch, 1986, p. 112). Both the nodes and the major linkages between them are capable of becoming memorable, imageable places within a city or city region.

The hierarchical structure of the composite city would allow the decentralisation of power and decision-making over development at town, district and neighbourhood level, with central administration providing the framework for decision-making at these different levels. The question of compactness of such a city depends on the amount of land included inside the net of linked neighbourhoods, districts and towns, which will be largely dependent upon existing conditions and the historical structure of the city. It would be naive to expect that the diagrammatic forms developed here could ever represent the true structure of a city because forms and sizes of neighbourhood and districts differ as a result of topographical factors or the specific historical development pattern of places. But if a city could be structured according to the principles of a hierarchical micro-structure with transport networks as integrators, the decentralisation of provisions into town, district and neighbourhood centres would diffuse traffic and solve many of the city's problems of congestion and consequent pollution. The proposed structure would work well with good and well co-ordinated public transport systems and would foster a considerable reduction of vehicular traffic inside developed areas. There may be many who question whether in view of the flexibility and comfort of the private car this can ever be achieved, particularly when the argument is taken into considera-

tion that cleaner types of fuel and the electric car, already under research if not introduced to the market in the USA, would solve the problem of pollution. But these solutions do not eliminate the other major problem: congestion of roads in the denser developed areas of cities and conurbations. If congestion caused by vehicular traffic were seriously tackled, as today in the UK it generally is not, then the proposed structure may provide a model that generates a more sustainable city and city region.

3.2 The Macro-structure of Alternative City Models

Investigation has so far concentrated on models that promise a high degree of user-friendliness in terms of mobility and access to services and facilities within walking and cycling distance and by public transport. This has led to a micro-structure with a hierarchy of different provision centres and different linkages between them. It is now important to compare different macro-structures that provide other qualities which depend upon the city's overall form and development pattern rather than the micro-structure within: a large number of different housing forms, good environmental conditions, a high degree of adaptability to changing needs and socio-economic conditions, access to open space for recreation and other functions, and access to the countryside. To classify city forms on these accounts requires accurate data of overall densities, total area required, minimum and maximum distances, etc., and these data are generated with the help of a number of theoretical city models.

There are a number of publications which discuss the spatial patterns and the distribution of uses of a better – in today's jargon, a 'more sustainable' – city. They rehearse alternative patterns, or city models, and evaluate them with a set of criteria, standards and performance values. Some of these publications deal with abstract, non-situation-specific city forms and establish their expected performance standards; others are based on the understanding that the task is not to find a new city structure but to improve the structure of our existing cities by asking how they should develop. All have a common starting point, the inefficiency of a mono-core city with sprawling suburbs, so typical of many of the post-industrial European and almost all of the older-generation US and Australian cities.

In the investigation of such models much emphasis must be given to the fact that the city is undergoing continuous adaptation to changing socio-economic conditions, that the city form is never finite, never completed, that it must allow adaptation and change to take place. It must be clear, however, that cities do not change radically and in their entirety but in their parts, in their districts, neighbourhoods and individual streets, squares and buildings. It seems to be one of the city's characteristics that its parts – maybe not all of them but some of them – undergo a period of growth and development and, after having reached the height of development, a period of decline followed by renewal and revitalisation to reach a new height to be followed by a new period of decline. The study of a city's history will reveal such fluctuations of districts and urban areas. Glasgow's Merchant City is a good example. The area developed first as a housing district for the better-off, then it developed into a city of merchants with a high concentration of warehouses and commerce, only to lose its role in the city with the development of heavy industry and decline to unimportance and dilapidation. But from the mid-1970s on it was revived and regenerated to become a mixed-use area of considerable attraction. City form must accommodate such change of districts without loss of the city's overall viability, identity and imageability.

The following discussion of urban form does not focus on details of form, of spaces and buildings and of a 'timeless' and 'natural' way of building, valid for all people and for all places and for all socio-economic conditions as suggested in Christopher Alexander's 'pattern language' (Alexander et al., 1975). The search here is for dynamic structures of the city that change to remain valid and stay alive.

As already indicated, a number of publications describe different city forms and structures and their characteristics. The most useful of these in this context include Kevin Lynch's *Good City Form* (Lynch, 1985, specifically Appendix A, pp. 373–455); Lynch's 'The Pattern of the Metropolis', in which he extends the analysis to city forms of metropolitan scale (Lynch, 1961 [1991], pp. 47–64); John Minnery's *Urban Form and Development Strategies*, in which he discusses different types of urban form and the development strategies used to achieve them (Minnery, 1992); and Calthorpe's *The Next American Metropolis*, which explains the concept of transit-oriented developments and their implementation in practice (Calthorpe, 1993).

Some models presented and evaluated in these publications share characteristics and cannot be ignored in this context. They are presented roughly in order of Lynch's catalogue of models of settlement form, with discussion of the macro-scale structure of such city models, and are all assumed to accommodate a similar total population beyond the comfortable scale, of say a quarter of a million or half a million people. Excluded are models of extreme low density which have to be considered as inappropriate regarding a more sustainable city form. Also excluded are models describing micro-scale patterns which could be the properties of any of the macro-scale models.

The comparison of different city forms and structures focuses first on those characteristics and performance values described by Lynch and the other authors. As these descriptions rarely provide accurate information

regarding the area and population of the individual models, the evaluation needs later to become more specific regarding size and area of each model for identical population densities. Then the city models are evaluated and compared on the basis of the generally agreed sustainability characteristics summarised at the end of section 2.2: the degree of containment of development; population density relative to the land needed; viability of public transport; dispersal of vehicular transport; viability of mixed uses; access to services and facilities; access to green open spaces; environmental conditions; the potential for social mix; the potential of local autonomy; the potential for self-sufficiency; the degree of adaptability of the city to changing needs and conditions; the imageability of the city models as a whole and of their districts; and the sense of place and centrality they provide.

The Core City

The core city model *(Fig. 3.12)* is perhaps the most extreme concept of a compact city in which all the city's functions are packed into one continuous body with very high density and an intense peak of activities at the centre. Lynch (1985, pp. 373–4) suggests that, owing to the compactness, the extension of the built-up area of the city would be relatively small in comparison with more fragmented models discussed later. In the absence of any more detailed description of the structural characteristics of this type of city by those supporting it, it is assumed that this model has characteristics similar to the centre of Paris inside the *périphérique*, which has continuous high density from core to edge and a distribution of services and facilities throughout the city's area right to the edge. This kind of city is clearly reminiscent of the medieval city *(Fig. 3.13)* though of much larger scale. Green spaces in the core city would generally be small and take the form of local pockets, supported perhaps by the intensive greening of some streets

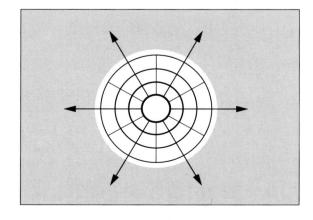

3–12. The core city

3–13. Mont-Saint-Michel in northern France

and squares. Housing would be predominantly in the form of multi-storey apartments rather than single-family houses, a limited number of which may locate in specific city districts. There would accordingly be only a limited variety of habitat.

According to Lynch, the core city would have high overall density of around 350 persons per hectare, which might generate discomfort in the form of noise and poor climate. Special activities and open country at the edges of the city would be highly accessible, and each family might have a second house in the country. There would be a highly specified system of almost entirely public transport rather than individual vehicles. There would be plentiful outdoor facilities in close proximity to housing. Distances between facilities, workplaces and residence would be short. The core city would be highly imageable and provide a strong sense of community, but the degree of flexibility would be low and there would be no potential for participation in local affairs. Some of these characteristics highlighted by Lynch seem to be contradictory and need to be verified later, specifically the claim of good access to the open country and of plentiful outdoor facilities, which seem to be somewhat questionable.

It is often said that major problems arise if the core city grows beyond a certain dimension and size of population because this would lead to increasing and eventually massive congestion, a high level of pollution and excessive land and property values which would make it socio-economically exclusive. If the compact city grows too big, the tendency to escape the city, maybe first with the help of a weekend cottage in the country, then into lower-density suburbs, would be hard to resist and likely to start the same decentralisation process the nineteenth-century city has witnessed unless dicta-

torial restrictions were in place to curb suburbanisation – which might be socially and politically unacceptable. However, it is difficult to find, in all the literature about the compact city, threshold values for density and size, maximum population and expansion, at which the core city starts to become problematic. It is also difficult to find comparisons of the land take of a compact city that includes agricultural and forestry land at its edge in amounts similar to those of more composite city forms. Such a comparison needs to be made after the main characteristics of other city models have been analysed.

The core city would, however, have undoubted advantages in the form of short distances and good access to facilities and the countryside if its size and accordingly its population remained relatively small; this is the main argument behind Howard's 'city cluster' concept, discussed later. But the question arises whether the limited size of population – in Howard's concept 32,000 for the Garden City and 58,000 for the Central City – would support all those services and facilities that make the large core city, like the city centre of Paris, so attractive. In comparative terms, would the centre of Paris provide so many services and facilities if the other Paris outside the *périphérique* did not exist? Hardly. Therefore, both the densities and dimensions of such a core city need to be investigated further and need to be compared with those of other city models; maybe Lynch's optimum population for satellite cities – between 25,000 and 250,000 inhabitants – might be appropriate for the core city as well. Another question might arise as to whether the smaller core city would have to become part of a larger whole composed of a number of such cities linked by public transport in order to support services and facilities beyond those provided by the individual cities themselves. But then we would no longer talk about a core city but a polycentric metropolitan area.

The Star City

Another of Lynch's city models is that of the 'star' (Lynch, 1985) or the 'urban star' (Lynch, 1961 [1991]) *(Fig. 3.14)*. It has a single dominant centre of high density and mixed uses. Transportation routes radiate out of the centre containing public transport systems and the main vehicular traffic routes. Secondary centres and other uses of high to medium density are located along the public transport routes with the more intensive uses around the subcentres which form at transport stops. Less intensive use may occupy space outside either side of the denser development along the routes, towards the green wedges. Tongues of open land, in which even low-density development would be disallowed, take up the space between the 'fingers' of linear development which is incorporated into the city area. At moderate densities (less than the core) the 'fingers' might extend considerably, even to other metropolitan centres. Concentric highways and public transport routes, at intervals outwards from the main centre, link the fingers but without accompanying development except at crossing points with radial routes. The centre would contain the most intensive types of city-wide activities; subcentres along the radial transport routes would have activities on a less intense level. Each family might have a second house in the country (a suggestion that seems to be at odds with the other statement that in the green wedges not even low-density development would be allowed). The transport flow would be organised on the radial pattern in the form of high-capacity public transport (primary system), with supplementary concentric rings and public transport of lower intensity (secondary system); vehicular traffic would follow other (not specified) directions. The main radials might become overloaded with continuing growth of the star. Choice of habitat

would be wide, access to services and open land good, but access to services unequal as between inner and outer locations. According to Lynch, area and size of the urban star can be expected to be more extensive in comparison with the core city because it includes a substantial amount of open land, ever increasing with growing city size. The advantage of the green wedges, however, would be that they reach right to the central core area. The star city of limited size can be expected to have a good visual image and sense of community as a whole and to be reasonably flexible as a result of the lower densities and the amount of open land incorporated.

This kind of city developed frequently as a result of the introduction of public transport (railway and tram-car) during the nineteenth and early twentieth centuries. The idea was exploited by Hans Blumenfeld (1949) and influenced the plan of Washington, the general plan of Moscow and that of Copenhagen *(Fig. 3.15)*. Transport and communication lines which form the basis of the city structure and form allow the city to become less car dependent. This was the major objective of Copenhagen's planners when in 1947 they adopted the 'finger plan', the concept of urban development along main transport lines which ensured that the travel time to the centre would be 30 minutes at the most (Hartoft-Nielson, 1993, p. 12). The concept also provides easy access to green open wedges which link the city to the country. In practice it may prove difficult to maintain the wedges as open, continuous green spaces, as the development of Copenhagen illustrates: during the years of rapid growth large tracts of open land were assigned to urban development far away from public transport but close to the green wedges and main highways (see Hartoft-Nielson, 1993, pp. 17–18).

The system is reasonably flexible as it can grow outward. However, growth must be limited in order to

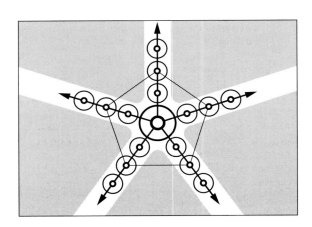

3–14. The star city

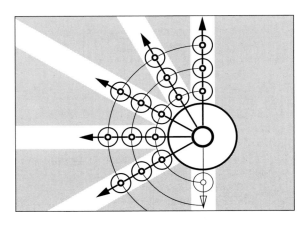

3–15. Diagrammatic representation of Copenhagen's 'finger plan' (based on original publication, 1947 from Hartoft-Nielson, 1993)

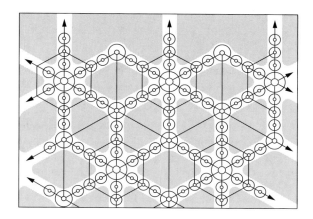

3–16. *Metropolitan multi-nucleated structure formed by linked star cities*

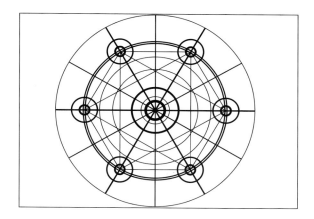

3–17. *Satellites around a central city: Howard's concept of 'garden cities of tomorrow' (based on Howard, 1898)*

avoid congestion of the centre and overloaded radial lines of transport. For city development of metropolitan size this structure is likely to be inefficient as it depends on one central core, but the star could be an element in a multi-centred structure in which several stars form a larger whole *(Fig. 3.16)*. The disadvantage of the resulting metropolitan structure is likely to be that the green spaces at least in the inner areas of the metropolis might no longer be continuously linked with the rural environment but trapped between fingers of development.

The Satellite City

In the satellite city model *(Fig. 3.17)* a central city is surrounded, at some distance, by a set of satellite communities of limited size (according to Lynch the optimum population of a satellite is between 25,000 and 250,000 inhabitants). Growth of the central city is channelled not into continuous development 'fingers' but into separate communities. The limitation of the growth of satellites is believed to be essential as beyond a certain size compact cities are generally thought to become less efficient and to provide poorer environmental and living conditions; when maximum size has been reached, another satellite is started. Satellites are separated from the central city by rural land and are themselves surrounded by greenbelts.

An important proponent of this city model was Ebenezer Howard with his *To-morrow: A Peaceful Path to Real Reform* (Howard, 1898), which Mumford claims to be the first valid approach to the problem of population numbers and containment (Mumford, 1984, p. 184). The concept of Howard's Garden City, much misunderstood even today, is based on the understanding that growth of the big city is, owing to increasing traffic congestion and difficulty of access to the centre, self-defeating. Howard presents a new pattern of city development, that of self-contained and self-sufficient but

linked centres, separated by agricultural land that supports them and provides the opportunity of a symbiosis with the natural environment. The model rejects the suburb as unacceptable compromise and achieves relief of congestion through decentralisation of all the city's functions. Each city is limited in size and in population density – 32,000 in the Garden City and 58,000 in the Central City of the 'city cluster' – and accommodates all the essential functions of an urban community: business, industry, administration, education, public parks and private gardens (Mumford, 1984, pp. 586–7).

In today's language Howard's concept of a city cluster has not only the characteristics of decentralised concentration but also those of the kind of city advocated by Patrick Geddes which integrates the country and the town (Geddes, 1915), and with it the properties of an eco-city. Mumford describes it as a 'town cluster' (Howard's term) set in a permanent green matrix, 'that would overcome the spatial limitations of the historic city, even that of the boundless expansion and random diffusion of the conurbation' (Mumford, 1984, p. 595).

But Howard not only developed a physical model of the structuring of metropolis; perhaps more importantly, he generated a model of an alternative society, 'neither capitalist nor bureaucratic socialist: a society based on a voluntary co-operation among men and women, working and living in small self-governing commonwealths' (Hall, 1990, p. 3). The Garden City embraces the concept of people creating their own built, economic and social environment. Thus Howard's concept responds to many of the characteristics of a sustainable city: decentralisation of the core city's functions to generate all needed local services and facilities in each Garden City, and in the farmland surrounding it; decentralisation of responsibility and participation of the communities in the process of shaping and building their own cities according to their needs and aspirations; a symbiotic relationship with the countryside; a considerable degree of open-endedness and flexibility of development; and virtually limitless growth of the pattern to any metropolitan size.

There are, however, some problems with Howard's concept. Development control would have to be strict to prevent the growth of a city beyond its limited size and population density and to prevent development in the surrounding farmland, both of which would destroy the functional and environmental balance between city and its hinterland. Furthermore, and more importantly, the limited size and population of each of the independent and self-sufficient cities would inevitably result in a rather limited range of services and facilities in individual cities because they do not create a higher-level entity with a higher-level provision centre, and this would have serious consequences for the quality of life in the 'city cluster'.

The satellite city concept has found numerous applications, for instance in Stretton's *Ideas for Australian Cities* (Stretton, 1971), Abercrombie's final plan of 1944 for Greater London (Abercrombie, 1945), or the new town strategy for Paris *(Fig. 3.18)*. In practice, the building of satellite cities, as in the cases of London and Paris, has not prevented the central city from continuing to grow, and it has been difficult to establish whether its growth would have been even greater without satellites. In Paris, the chosen distances between the central city and the satellites were not sufficient to prevent the area in between becoming almost entirely developed, rendering the satellite concept ineffective. New towns around Glasgow have also clearly shown that the size of the central city and the distance between new town and central city are crucial for a satellite to work as an independent entity; the case of Cumbernauld shows that this new town is located too close to Glasgow and also shows that a satellite must have appropriate services

and facilities to satisfy the demands of the population. Cumbernauld cannot compete with Glasgow's considerable retail core, which draws people like a magnet into the old city centre; and the distance is short enough to get to the old centre within a 20 to 30 minute bus ride. This in turn may well mean that the development of satellites is only really viable in economic and functional terms if the central city is only marginally larger than the satellites and offers little more than their cores; but then the restriction of services and facilities would reduce the quality in the central city and the satellites unless a hierarchy of provision centres could be included in the structure.

The Galaxy of Settlements

Lynch's galaxy of settlements represents an urban or metropolitan form in which the old centre and subcentres of today's city are, as the result of continued decentralisation, dispersed into small units, each with a relatively dense central core and linked by a network of communication and transport lines *(Fig. 3.19)*. The units would be separated by areas of either low-density development (suburbia) or open land. According to Lynch, the galaxy of settlements would have low median density and would require 30–50% more area than an equivalent city or metropolis of today even with minimum inter-spaces. The centres of units might be relatively equal in importance as city-wide activities are dispersed into the density peaks of individual units. Low overall density would also mean that circulation would be predominantly by private car with traffic converging at the centre of each unit. There may be some supplementary public transport, e.g. by buses. There would be a limited range of mixed uses in the cores of the units with their other areas predominantly for housing; workplaces and residence would either be close by or miles apart and dependency upon a central city would be

Cergy-Pointoise

Roissy/
Charles de Gaulle

Marne-la-
Vallée

St Quentin-en-
Yvelines

Evry

3–18. *The satellite cities of Paris: diagrammatic plan (based on a tourist map)*

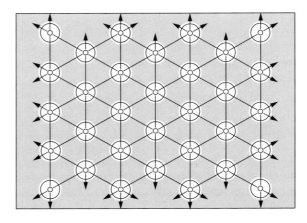

3–19. *The galaxy of settlements (based on Lynch's representation of this metropolitan model)*

high. The units would provide a larger variety of house types from high-density low-rise at the cores around traffic nodes and low-density family units towards the edge of and in areas in between units. There would be plenty of outdoor facilities in close proximity to housing; green spaces would vary, ranging from fragmented pockets between units to open countryside.

In contrast to Lynch's 'dispersed sheet' or Minnery's spread cities (Minnery, 1992, pp. xvi, 20–1, 105–7) – in which all old centre and subcentre activities would be dissolved in a very low-density and entirely car-dependent suburbia without any specific focal point, like in Wright's Broadacre City, a concept eliminated from this investigation as it has to be regarded as highly unsustainable – the galaxy of settlements has some nodal structure with higher-density development around the nodes. If these nodes achieved medium to high average density development of pedestrian scale, say in a node of about a 600 m radius, they could serve as 'oases in the desert of suburbs' and might be effectively linked by public transport lines.

This concept would then resemble Calthorpe's transit-oriented developments (TODs; Calthorpe, 1993) *(Fig. 3.20)*, or Duany and Plater-Zyberk's traditional neighbourhood developments (TNDs), examples of 'neo-traditionalist' developments in the USA under the label 'new urbanism' (Duany and Plater-Zyberk, 1991), or in fact 'urban villages' (Urban Villages Group, 1992), the first two conceived as alternative to urban sprawl,

the latter as new free-standing settlements in the UK. Calthorpe's TODs would have the following characteristics (Calthorpe, 1993, pp. 65–71):

- approximate size of a TOD 80 ha;

- distance from edge to centre 10 minutes' walk (about 600 m);

- a fine grain of different land uses; in an urban TOD two-thirds of the area would be housing, one-third commercial and workplaces; with an average residential density of 44.5 dwelling units per hectare up to 6,000 people would be accommodated (average family size assumed to be 2.5 persons); a neighbourhood TOD would be less dense and accommodate up to 3,000 people;

- a central area operates as the focus of the community's activities, with a public transport stop, shops, restaurants and services, some small businesses, a community, a local library and perhaps a crèche facility and a small public square or park; towards the edge of the core area there may also be a primary school;

- residential development in the central area would be in the form of high-density low-rise apartments or town houses, beyond that in the form of lower-density terraces or row houses, all within 10 minutes' walk of the centre and a few minutes' walk only from a local playground;

- an area of up to 1,600 m from the central public transport stop would provide lower-density single-family housing, public recreation space, parks with ponds, and countryside.

Calthorpe describes the TODs as 'a modern version of the traditional town' (Calthorpe, 1993, p. 16), but their limited size and, accordingly, limited population make them more like traditional 'villages' than 'towns', which may provide for as many day-to-day needs as possible but not for much more. Though accommodating some workplaces and commerce and some local services and facilities, TODs and TNDs certainly do not represent independent entities like Howard's social cities with a population of 32,000 and all workplaces and facilities within the city and its hinterland. The question arises therefore whether these models, which address suburban sprawl rather than the structure of metropolis, are generally applicable. With an average population of up to 3,000 (neighbourhood TODs) and 6,000 (urban TODs) (Calthorpe, 1993, pp. 57–8), the viability of public transport may be questionable and car dependency is likely to continue (see Thomas and Cousins, 1996, p. 330). It is also evident that TODs and TNDs, like neighbourhoods in new towns in the UK, will not be self-sufficient in terms of provisions and it is more than likely that the majority of their inhabitants will depend upon a

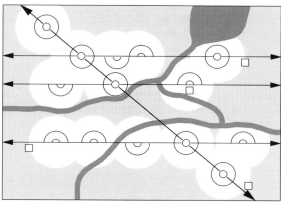

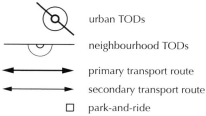

3–20. Calthorpe's transit-oriented developments (TODs) (based on Calthorpe, 1993, p. 42)

central metropolitan or regional city when it comes to workplaces and the provision of services and facilities beyond day-to-day needs. Therefore, such small units or neighbourhoods cannot be seen in isolation but should be part of a more complex structure with different kinds of centres, each with different kinds of provisions, as already discussed (see section 3.1).

The Linear City

The linear city form *(Fig. 3.21)* has frequently been debated and put forward as a dynamic alternative to the more static core city. Some of the best-known plans are those by Soria y Mata for Madrid (*La ciudad lineal*, first published in 1882, then as a detailed proposal in 1892, a linear garden city growing out of the city along a public transport system); Edgar Chambless's 'Roadtown'; Clarence Stein's proposals; and the MARS group's proposals for London.

The linear city grows along a continuous transport line, ideally public transport, or a parallel series of lines. Intensive uses of production, residence, commerce and services are located along and on either side of the line(s) and, specifically, form dense nodes at transport stops. Less intensive uses are located in parallel bands of space outside the compact strips of development. Rural land is immediately beyond the less dense bands and in close proximity to all development, which is relatively shallow. Overall the linear city is compact but has no central core. There would be relatively equal access to services, jobs and open land, though areas between transport stops are likely to be less well served than areas around a transport node. The public transport system would be efficient as the city form follows its linear nature. There would be a reasonably good mixture of uses in the band of intensive uses and around transport stops, and a considerable variety of housing is possible ranging from high-density low-rise along the linear centre and around transport stops to single family homes at

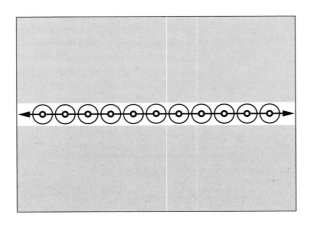

3–21. The linear city

the city's edge to the open country. Growth would be possible by linear extension at either end of the line; adaptability inside the linear city would be by replacement as in all other denser city models. The green space outside and in parallel to the linear city would provide the opportunity of a balanced relationship between city and country and provide a degree of self-sufficiency.

Mayer Hillman argues that the concept of the linear city is based on the conviction that the quality of life in the city could be greatly enhanced if car dependency could be reduced (Hillman, 1996, p. 42). Commercial facilities, services and workplaces as well as green open spaces could be within walking distance from housing areas, thus greatly reducing the need to travel. The linear form results from 'the inevitable linear nature of public transport systems' (Scoffham and Vale, 1996, p. 72).

The linear city concept is rarely implemented except in the familiar form of a commercial strip as in Las Vegas or between traditional towns and cities as, notably, in France *(Fig. 3.22)* and Italy. One attempt to generate a linear city must, however, be referred to: the new town of Cumbernauld near Glasgow *(Fig. 3.23)*. In contrast to all other new towns in the UK, this one is based not on a neighbourhood structure but on a linear centre, expandable at both ends and accommodating all city centre functions, flanked on both sides by villages within walking distance of the linear centre. Consistent with 1960s thinking, the concept is based on private vehicular rather than public transport, which makes links between different city areas car dependent but would not be so problematic for the links between housing and central facilities if the original concept of villages parallel, and with pedestrian access, to the linear centre had been adhered to. Unfortunately the original site survey ignored mining problems in areas designated for housing which later rendered economic construction impossible and caused villages to be constructed much further away from the linear centre, making access to those facilities that are not provided in the villages, but only by the linear centre, dependent upon the car.

Reasons why the linear city is rarely implemented may well be that this form of development requires massive investment in efficient public transport and related infrastructure and may become effective and economically viable only in the form of cross-city links (Minnery, 1992, pp. xv, 98–101). An example of the application of the linear city concept is Kurokawa's Tokyo 2025 proposal with two linear loops on the mainland and another linear strip forming an oval on an artificial island in Tokyo Bay (Kurokawa, 1987, pp. 46–63). The proposal also contains the formation of a metropolitan corridor linking Tokyo, Nagoya, Kyoto and Osaka with a new railway system. The corridor would enable the partial dispersion of the functions of the capital city, and would form a unified information system (Kurokawa, 1987, p. 55). A similar configuration is provided with

3–22. Commercial strip at Nîmes, France

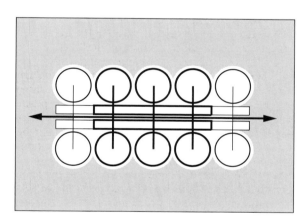

3–23. Diagrammatic representation of the original concept of Cumbernauld new town

The Polycentric Net or the Regional City

Lynch's polycentric net resembles a dispersed form of the metropolis with a specialised and complex circulation system taking on the form of a triangular grid pattern that can grow in any direction. There is a wide range of different densities, with intensive peaks at junctions of the transport network and with high linear concentrations along the major channels between the peaks. Inside the grid, or between high-density nodes and linear development, would be large regions of low density. Green belts and wedges would form another kind of grid *(Fig. 3.24)*. It is obvious that this city or metropolitan model is a composite form of other city models. Central city activities would be decentralised over the net and concentrated in nodes at junctions of the circulation system with different densities and degrees of

another growth-region or growth-corridor concept, the proposal of a polynucleated 'Park City' between The Hague, Zoetermeer and Rotterdam (van der Valk and Faludi, 1992, pp. 129–30). Both the Japanese metropolitan corridor and the 'Park City' plans represent a macro-scale pattern of linked cities in a linear metropolitan region rather than an individual linear city. Perhaps it is at this macro-scale, at which the 'linear city' does not occur independently from other development (as for instance in Cumbernauld) but forms linkages between existing cities or growth centres, that the linear development concept proves to be more suitable and more realistic than the linear city on its own. When several different linear development directions coincide, the linear city concept changes into that of a polycentric net, which will be investigated in due course.

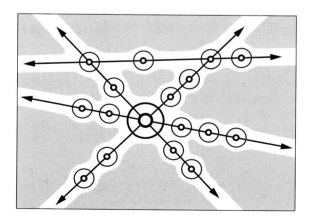

3–24. The polycentric net or regional city

specialisation; there would be larger and smaller centres, the first more specialised. Between the major nodes dense linear cities might develop along transport lines; away from such dense nodes and linear development the network would thin out and adapt to local configurations and topography. There would be a large range of different housing forms and a large choice of access to services and open land. Between nodal and linear development would be open country and parks.

This polycentric net basically represents a combination of larger and smaller core and linear cities or a combination of urban stars and shows the characteristics, structure and form of a regional city, except that a regional city may not necessarily have a central metropolitan core (Minnery, 1992, pp. xv, 19–20, 101–4). Such a form would offer a large variety of different centres and different living conditions; equity, choice and variety would therefore be improved and access to cores would be good by car (for those living in low-density areas between cores and linear cities), by foot or bicycle (for those living around cores or in linear cities) and by public transport (for all those living close to the circulation network). This form of city would preserve nature reserves and important open spaces, as its geometry can adapt to local conditions.

3.3 Comparison of Areas and Dimensions of the City Models

So far few and rather vague assumptions have been made regarding the land required by each city model to accommodate the same number of people. The general consensus seems to be that the core city requires the least amount of land and therefore helps preserve the countryside, but no figures are available as to whether this is true in practice, and so I shall proceed to calculate the land required by the various city models. Excluded from this comparison is the galaxy of settlements, because of its high degree of dispersal, which cannot be the model for a sustainable form of city or city region (though the neighbourhood does play a part in the micro-structure of the city). Also excluded is the polycentric net, as it represents a composite of other urban forms; its performance may depend on its actual configuration but can be assumed to be similar to that of the city models of which it is composed. In the following a comparison is made of the dimensions and the overall city areas of the core city, the star and the satellite city and the linear city. In order to achieve comparability, the study is based on the following conditions:

- The overall area of a city to include open country; the amount to be 40% of the total area, with 60% built-up area (including streets, squares, pocket parks, etc.). This proportion follows the Chinese city model though with the smallest percentage of farmland and forestry

included in the city's administrative area, but still able to render the city largely self-sufficient regarding the production of vegetables and meat as long as soil and climatic conditions are favourable. In Glasgow, of all areas included within the administrative boundary the countryside is 22%, vacant land 10% and the built-up area 68% of the total city area; the latter includes public parks and gardens (information obtained from the City of Glasgow Council Planning Department). The overall relationship between built-up and open land may therefore be around 60% to 40%.

- The average gross population density (the number of persons per hectare (pph) of city area *excluding* open countryside) to be 60 pph. Again, the actual density could be higher or lower and does not really matter all that much in this calculation, as will become clear later, but for comparative purposes a density has been selected which achieves a sufficiently high population in neighbourhoods and districts to support their respective central function. This figure is also similar to Howard's Garden City, which accommodates 32,000 people on 405 ha, the area designated for the Social City, and achieves a respectable gross population density of 79 pph (a fact very frequently ignored when Howard's Garden City is falsely classified as garden suburb, which would have a gross population density only of somewhere between 10 and 40 pph). Some of the people of a social city may actually live in the surrounding country and the actual population of the city may be somewhat lower. A population density of 60 pph is also the kind of middle ground in a city like Glasgow – which varies between 10 to 120 pph with an overall gross population density of 35.09 pph over the total city area (Glasgow City Council, 1995). Assuming that about 40% of the city's area is not built upon (open space, forests, etc.), then the net population density is around 58.5 pph, which is close to the 60 pph chosen as threshold value.

- Each model to accommodate a population of 250,000 and 500,000 respectively; this will allow an insight into the changing land requirements and dimensions of each city model as a result of doubling the population. Other and larger population figures could have been chosen, but with fixed gross population density and a standard amount of open land included in the city area the overall dimensions of city models are likely not to vary significantly with increasing or decreasing population; they only get larger or smaller. Therefore the actual population is of little significance, particularly when considering composite city models like the satellite, the galaxy of settlements, the polycentric net, which can grow to metropolitan size and several million inhabitants. A more limited population has been chosen to test the performance specifically of the core city. The upper population size of 500,000 is close to the populations of Copenhagen, Zürich, Glasgow, cities already mentioned and of importance in this context, and the first figure (Lynch's maximum population of a satellite city)

may prove a threshold for the viability of some models beyond which they may no longer work efficiently within the given conditions.

• For the dispersed city models – the star and the satellite city – the population accommodated in the central city to be about 23% of the total city population, with 77% in the 'fingers' or satellites. This distribution follows that of Howard's Garden City and makes sure that the central city is only proportionally larger so that the satellites are at least semi-autonomous.

On the basis of these conditions the dimensions of each city model are calculated for the two population sizes. *Figures 3.25–3.28* show the city configurations in diagrammatic form and the cities' dimensions. Regarding the micro-structure of the city models, all have a hierarchical composition with neighbourhoods forming districts, districts forming towns and towns forming the city. But there are some differences. The central area of the core city *(Fig. 3.25)* cannot be expected to show clearly differentiated neighbourhoods, districts and towns as development is continuous and of the same or similar density and compactness. Neighbourhoods and districts may be there in the concentration of specific uses or a specific spatial or formal configuration, but they may overlap, and facilities as well as services may be distributed throughout the central area. Only towards the edge of the city may neighbourhoods, districts and towns form a visible structure. The central towns of the star *(Fig. 3.26)* and satellite city *(Fig. 3.27)* have a similar structure to that of the core city and show no clearly visible hierarchy, though one may actually exist. But the fingers, and to a degree the satellites, may show groups of neighbourhoods and of districts. In the smaller star city the fingers are formed by districts along the concentric transport routes; those of the larger star city may be formed by towns. This differentiation is the result of the space provision around the smaller and larger central town. The linear city *(Fig. 3.28)* too has to some degree a hierarchical structure in the form of a linear configuration of districts as agglomerations of neighbourhoods. An arrangement of this city model as agglomeration of towns is excluded as this would require a complex secondary transport network, which would contradict the linearity of development along one major transport route. The consistency of hierarchical composition makes sure that all centres have the same or similar access and catchment areas, but in the core city this composition is not clearly visible. Each of the models is represented to the same scale to allow a comparison of their dimensions. *Table 3.01* documents the areas and dimensions of the four cities under comparison.

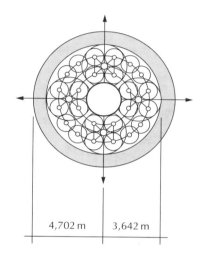

(a)

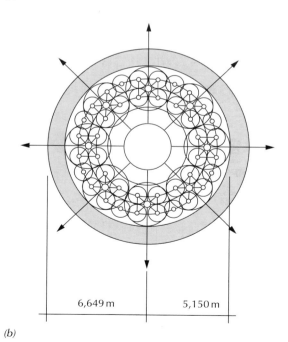

(b)

3–25. *Comparison of required area and dimensions of the core city: (a) population 250,000; (b) population 500,000*

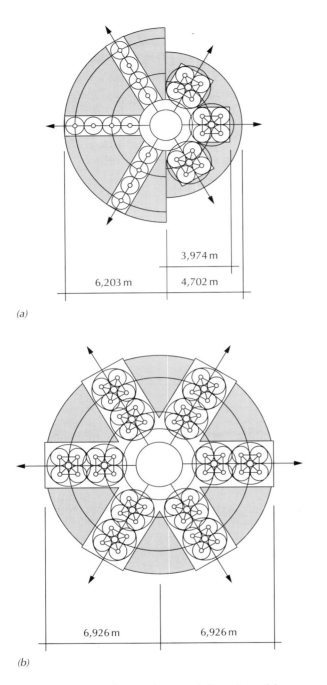

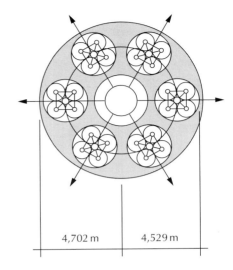

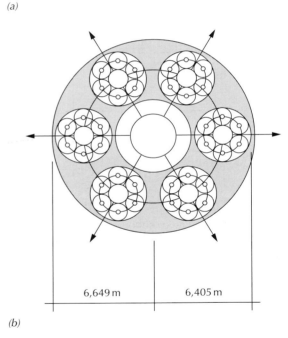

3–26. Comparison of required area and dimensions of the star city: (a) population 250,000 with finger width 1,200 and 2,400 m; (b) population 500,000 with finger width 2,400 m only

Areas and Dimensions of City Models with a Population of 250,000

At a population of 250,000, the core and satellite city and the linear city are identical in overall area required as well as the size of built-up area and open land; the

3–27. Comparison of required area and dimensions of the satellite city: (a) population 250,000; (b) population 500,000

star has the same built-up area but needs 5,143 ha more open land than the other cities if the depth of its fingers is 1,200 m. If the finger depth is increased to 2,400 m the star city's overall area becomes identical with that of all the other city models.

Distances between the edge of the built-up area and the centre differ considerably as a result of the different geometry and fragmentation of the urban fabric; the best values are achieved by the linear city (1,200 m with the depth of development 2,400 m) and the core city (3,642 m), the worst by the star (6,203 m with the

Table 3–01. Comparison of land take and dimensions – matrix (built-up area 60%, open land 40%)

Population 250,000		Core city	Star city finger $d = 1,200$ m	Star city finger $d = 2,400$ m	Satellite	Linear city $d = 2,400$ m
Total land required	(ha)	6,945	12,088	6,945	6,945	6,945
	(%)	100%	100%	100%	100%	100%
Built-up area	(ha)	4,167	4,167	4,167	4,167	4,167
	(%)	60%	34.5%	60%	60%	60%
Open land	(ha)	2,778	7,921	2,778	2,778	2,778
	(%)	40%	65.5%	40%	40%	40%
Distance centre to edge of built-up area	(m)	3,642	6,203	3,974	4,529	1,200
Distance centre to edge of city area	(m)	4,702	6,203	4,702	4,702	2,000
Tot. dimension city (diameter/length)	(m)	$d = 9,404$	$d = 12,406$	$d = 9,404$	$d = 9,404$	$l = 17,363$
Max. distance from built-up area to open land	(m)	3,642	1,746	1,746	1,746	1,200

Population 500,000		Core city	Star city finger $d = 2,400$ m	Satellite $d = 2,400$ m	Linear city $d = 2,400$ m
Total land required	(ha)	13,888	15,070	13,888	13,888
	(%)	100%	100%	100%	100%
Built-up area	(ha)	8,333	8,333	8,333	8,333
	(%)	60%	55.3%	60%	60%
Open land	(ha)	5,555	6,737	5,555	5,555
	(%)	40%	44.7%	40%	40%
Distance centre to edge of built-up area	(m)	5,150	6,926	6,405	1,200
Distance centre to edge of city area	(m)	6,649	6,926	6,649	2,000
Tot. dimension city (diameter/length)	(m)	$d = 13,298$	$d = 13,852$	$d = 13,298$	$l = 34,721$
Max. distance from built-up area to open land	(m)	5,150	2,470	2,470	1,200

depth of development of the fingers 1,200 m). However, when maximum distances between any point in the city and the edge of the open country are compared, the ranking order is rather different: the linear city is best (1,200 m), followed closely by the star and satellite city (1,754 m), and the core city has the largest distance (3,642 m).

Despite the good scoring of the linear city, the picture changes when overall dimensions of the city areas are compared; the diameters of the core and satellite city and the galaxy of settlements are best (9,404 m), followed by the star (12,406 m) with a finger depth of 1,200 m; with a finger depth of 2,400 m the star's diameter becomes identical to that of the core and satellite city. The linear city has a length of 17,363 m, which clearly indicates that this form is not suitable for a large population.

Areas and Dimensions of City Models with a Population of 500,000

At a population of 500,000, the core, satellite city and the linear city are again identical in overall area as well as the size of built-up area and open land. The star has the same built-up area, but even with a finger depth of 2,400 m it would still require 1,182 ha more land, owing to the length of the fingers. This indicates that with extension the star includes between the fingers an

Population 250,000

17,363 m

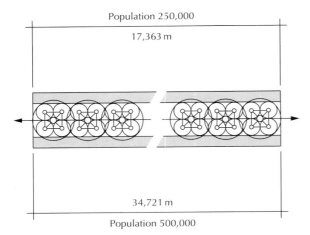

34,721 m

Population 500,000

3–28. Comparison of the required area and the plan form of the linear city for a population of 250,000 and 500,000

exponentially increasing amount of open land, which can be prevented to a degree by increasing the depth of the fingers; but this in turn requires a secondary transport system in the 'fingers' to get people from neighbourhoods to district centres, and such a more complex transport system may be less feasible. This clearly indicates that the star form is suitable only if the length of the 'fingers' is kept reasonably short.

Distances between the edge of the built-up area and the centre again differ considerably as a result of the divergent geometry and fragmentation of the urban fabric; the best values are achieved by the linear city (1,200 m) and the core city (5,150 m), the worst by the star and the satellite (6,926 m and 6,649 m respectively).

However, when maximum distances between any point in the city and the edge of the open country are compared, the ranking order is rather different: the linear city is best (1,200 m), followed closely by the star and satellite city (2,470 m); the core city has the largest distance (5,150 m). The diameters of the core, star and satellite city are equal (13,852 m). The linear city has a rather impracticable length of 34,722 m, which reinforces the argument that it is viable only when bridging short distances between different development centres.

The comparison shows that the linear city is not suitable on its own, but when linking core cities (like the fingers in a combination of stars, for instance) it may have its justification provided its length is limited. The star city is viable if the length of its fingers is kept reasonably short; up to a population of about 500,000 and with a finger depth of 2,400 m the star performs nearly as well as the satellite city. The cities differ with regard to maximum distance between edges of built-up areas and centre, which is understandably larger in the star and satellite city because of the decentralisation or fragmentation of urban fabric. They also differ with regard to the maximum distance between any point of the

built-up area and the edge of the open land, which is much shorter in the star and satellite city in comparison to the core city. The core city has shorter distances within the built-up area because it is compact, but has larger distances to open land because the open land is at the edge of development, not in between.

Regarding the compactness or fragmentation of the urban fabric in the core, star and satellite city, it becomes clear that it does not necessarily affect the amount of land required for the entire city as long as a stable percentage of open land is included in the city area. If this is the case, as was assumed in the comparison of city models, then the nature of the compact city debate changes considerably:

- With an identical percentage of open land included, the total area of the city models is identical or at least very similar; so is the percentage relationship between built-up and open areas. As a result of this and of identical average densities, the gross population density is therefore the same in all models.

- The decisive difference between the city models is then no longer the overall density of population but the degree of fragmentation or concentration of the built-up area and, as a consequence of that, better or worse access to, and more or less fragmentation of, the open land and a higher or lower degree of decentralisation of services and facilities.

If the conditions of the inclusion of the same amount of open land in the city area and the same average population density are fulfilled, the evaluation of city models can focus on performance values other than population densities, such as access to open land and degree of fragmentation of the open land. The question of the degree of compactness or fragmentation of the urban fabric too can be seen from another angle: the degree to which it facilitates mobility without congestion. And with these issues in mind, neither the core city with complete concentration of the urban fabric nor the galaxy of settlements with complete decentralisation of the urban fabric into something like neighbourhoods can any longer be considered as a preferred option. If these two city models are judged to perform worse than the other models – the compact city because of the likelihood of congestion, lack of privacy and personal outdoor space and large distances to the open country, the galaxy of settlements because of the lack of core areas with services and facilities of a higher order than those of the neighbourhood and with increased distances between built-up areas – the remaining models all exemplify a moderate degree of decentralised concentration which provides similar functional, social and environmental qualities almost regardless of the overall size of population.

3.4 Comparison of the Potential Performance of the Six City Models in Terms of Sustainability Indicators

It is now necessary to return to a more comprehensive set of evaluation criteria and to compare the city models with regard to all those properties which it is largely agreed that a more sustainable city should have. All city forms are included, despite the findings regarding land areas and dimensions which indicate that neither the star nor the linear city is suitable for large populations and that the linear city cannot really stand on its own but may become part of a composite form, linking core areas of a multi-nucleated city.

It is essential to keep in mind that the city models all represent macro-scale forms; they are concerned with the overall compactness or dispersal of urban fabric and with it the concentration or decentralisation of services, facilities and workplaces within the overall city form. But to this point no detailed investigation of the effects of this concentration or dispersal has been made. This, however, means that the macro-scale characteristics of the models have to be taken into consideration. An evaluation is therefore carried out as a matter of principle rather than detail. Furthermore, this evaluation is not scientific and not based on accurate measurements – for which the available empirical data are insufficient – but is based on reasonable assumptions regarding the influence of specific characteristics of urban form and structure on the city's overall performance. The actual degree to which the cities are more or less sustainable requires the models to provide clear and detailed specifications, and these need to be verified in later research.

What is known at this stage is that the core city, the satellite city, the galaxy of settlements and most likely also combinations of smaller stars or a multi-nucleated 'city net' offer more or less the same advantages in terms of areas required and overall dimensions. But there are some differences. One is that the core city, though offering shorter distances within the built-up areas, has not quite such a good relationship to the open country and may therefore not provide the same environmental quality as other models. Another is that the galaxy of settlements may provide open land that, because of the high degree of fragmentation of the urban fabric, is rather fragmented itself and perhaps not quite so suitable for forestry and agriculture and other larger-scale uses. Other similarities and differences emerge from the evaluation of the various city models, which is presented in tabular form (Tables 3.02 to 3.07).

A summary of the evaluation is again presented in matrix form. A simple scoring method is used, with sim-ple values varying from good (+) to indifferent or neither good nor bad (+/−) to bad (−). For each criterion the evaluation is summarised in a single such value, which is then aggregated to a total (Table 3.08). This comparison helps to provide a visual picture of the potential performance values of the six city models.

Overall, and under the assumption that all models accommodate a similar population and that all criteria are given equal weight, the core city scores worst, the linear city and the galaxy of settlements second worst, the star city is somewhere in the middle, and the satellite city and regional city score best. However, if the degree of containment, access to services and facilities, access to the countryside, environmental conditions and the potential for social mix, local autonomy and adaptability are given higher priorities, the core city clearly scores negatively in all aspects other than containment, the galaxy of settlements and the linear city are somewhere in the middle, the star city and satellite city score well and the regional city again scores best. If containment is given high priority, then the compact city scores best, and the galaxy of settlements and the linear city score worst, as can be expected. With regard to the city–country relationship, the core city is problematic when larger than the central core of the star or satellite city whereas all other city models score well.

The above exercise may be considered by some as crude, certainly superficial and perhaps even dangerous. However – in view of the confusion regarding the discussion of the values and deficiencies of different city models – the evaluation has been able to show that the inclusion of environmental and ecological criteria in the comparison of the city models changes the focus of the discussion of the 'compact city'. Population densities and containment of the urban fabric become relative values when seen against access to provision centres and to the open country, against environmental conditions, the potential for social mix and local autonomy and the degree of the adaptability of the city to changing needs and conditions. The question of a sustainable city form is therefore changed into the question of a sustainable regional form as it becomes increasingly clear that the quest for sustainability has to take into consideration not only that of the city but also that of the countryside with which the city ought to have a symbiotic relationship. The fact that the city models all score reasonably well under different weighting may actually mean that all of them may well play, on their own or in combination, a role in a sustainable city region and that the quality of the micro-structure may be more significant than that of the macro-structure.

Table 3–02. Evaluation of the performance of city models based on agreed sustainability characteristics: core city

Characteristics	Performance of city model
Degree of containment of development	The urban fabric is highly compact and continuous from centre to edge of this city model. There are only small pockets of green space. Open land is not incorporated in between the urban fabric but surrounds the core city.
Population density relative to land needed	The gross population density may be similar or identical to that of other city models but, owing to the compactness of the urban fabric, population is concentrated. There may be a variety of densities from very high at the centre of the core city to medium at its borders with the countryside.
Viability of public transport	The provision of primary and secondary public transport systems will be viable in all areas of the core city as a result of the concentration of people; it can even be expected to be necessary in order to reduce or eliminate road congestion. The systems might become congested in the central area of this city model owing to the high concentration of city-wide activities.
Dispersal of vehicular traffic	As a consequence of the high concentration of population, primary vehicular traffic would be likely to be increasingly concentrated into a number of major routes (likely to be radials and rings) the larger the city is. This would lead to increasing congestion; the use of the car would therefore have to be restricted in the core city, at least in its central area. All secondary traffic routes should be traffic-calmed to avoid adversary effects for developed areas.
Viability of mixed uses	There is a considerable potential for mixed uses throughout the core city as a consequence of the compactness of the urban fabric and the concentration of population. The centre of the core city may accommodate a peak of city-wide activities; a smaller variety of uses may locate towards the edges.
Access to services and facilities	Owing to the containment of the urban fabric and of the population in the core city, access to services and facilities, especially for daily and weekly use, may be expected to be rather good and distances short. With increasing size and population, access to the central area and its city-wide facilities is, however, likely to become increasingly difficult as transport routes become congested.
Access to green open spaces (parks, countryside)	As only smaller parks are included in the core city, access to green open areas can be expected to be rather poor from the more central areas but good at the edge of the core city. Distances to the surrounding countryside will be reasonable only as long as the core city is of limited size; but with growing size and population distances become even greater. A symbiotic relationship with nature is generally possible but limited to areas at the city edge as access to the country from the central areas becomes more problematic with increasing size and population of the city.
Environmental conditions (noise, pollution, congestion)	Open land at the city edge does not contribute sufficiently to the improvement of the inner-city environmental conditions as air drawn from the countryside (heat dome) becomes increasingly polluted on the way into the central area. Increasing the size and population of this city model may cause growing discomfort in the form of noise, poor climate and environmental conditions as well as lack of privacy and personal outdoor space.
Potential for social mix through variety of housing	Social mix may be viable only with heavy subsidies for social housing. One reason is that there is a reduced potential for a larger variety of dwelling types in a continuously developed urban environment. Another reason is that land and property values in the core city model can be expected to be generally high. The core city is therefore likely to be socially exclusive unless the lower-income groups are supported.
Potential for local autonomy	The density and complexity of the city model are likely to prevent a high degree of participation by communities in the shaping of their own environment unless the city's micro-structure shows some form of hierarchical decomposition of the built-up area into community territories which will then allow a degree of localised autonomy.
Potential for self-sufficiency	Self-sufficiency can be achieved if, as in most traditional Chinese cities, a sufficient amount of country in the form of farmland and forests is included in the city's administrative area. The hinterland, surrounding the core city and without fragmentation, can effectively serve for a large variety of different uses.
Degree of adaptability	The high concentration of urban fabric reduces the city's adaptability to changing conditions and change is possible only by replacement.
Imageability of the city (the physical entity) as a whole	With limited size, the core city is likely to be highly imageable owing to its compact form. With growing population the imageability of the city as a whole is, however, likely to become increasingly difficult.
Imageability of parts of the city (neighbourhoods, districts, towns)	The identity of districts in the core city can be expected to require careful design attention as there is a tendency towards continuous fabric with little variety. The generation of imageable districts may be aided through the concentration of specific uses into different areas.
Sense of place and centrality	The core city is likely to have a good sense of place and centrality in its centre (usually the historical core), but surrounding areas need to be designed to have clearly distinguishable features and subcentres.

Table 3–03. Evaluation of the performance of city models based on agreed sustainability characteristics: star city

Characteristics	Performance of city model
Degree of containment of development	Compactness can be achieved in the central core and the 'fingers' but – like the satellite city model – the star city incorporates open land, in this model in between the 'fingers'. Accordingly the urban fabric is fragmented though continuous in its development from core to the ends of the 'fingers'.
Population density relative to land needed	The gross population density is similar or identical to that of other city models but population is dispersed into a central city and 'fingers' and therefore less concentrated. The central city may have a somewhat higher density than the 'fingers', but there will hardly be any variation between the 'fingers'. There may be a variety of densities from very high in the central area and around nodes along the 'fingers' to medium at the edge of the central city and 'fingers' to the country.
Viability of public transport	A primary public transport system would be viable as a result of the concentration of urban fabric along major radial centre-oriented transport routes. Concentric links between fingers would be less efficient as only fractions of one 'finger' are connected with fractions of another; these connections may therefore depend upon the car. Inside the central city a secondary transport system may be necessary and viable owing to the concentration of population; in the 'fingers' a secondary system may be less viable but might be essential if development is deeper.
Dispersal of vehicular traffic	Primary vehicular transport routes are likely to be concentrated in the development 'fingers' and in concentric rings linking fingers. Whereas no major problems may arise in the rings, with growing size of the city traffic along the 'finger' spines would cause considerable congestion and pollution, especially in the central city where traffic routes converge; the use of the car may therefore have to be largely restricted inside the central core area.
Viability of mixed uses	There is good potential for mixed uses in the core and around transport nodes along the radial routes. In the core a larger variety of uses can be accommodated; the fingers may have a more limited potential for mixed use, which may be accommodated at the traffic nodes.
Access to services and facilities	The city centre will accommodate a large variety of different city-wide activities whereas the nodes along the 'fingers' are likely to provide for daily and weekly needs only. There is good access from most development areas to the city centre and to secondary centres, but access to city-wide activities is better closer to the city centre.
Access to green open spaces (parks, countryside)	All areas in the 'fingers' can be considered to have good access to the green wedges; in the central city distances to the open land vary between core and edge locations, and the proportion of land to the adjacent population is smallest at the edge of the central city. Because of the reasonably short distance a symbiotic relationship of all areas with nature is, however, possible.
Environmental conditions (noise, pollution, congestion)	Owing to the extension of the open countryside into the wedges between 'fingers' and right to the edge of the core, the environmental conditions are likely to be good as fresh air is drawn towards the centre via the wedges. Conditions will be better in the fingers than in the central city, which is more compact. Increased size of the city may, however, cause some discomfort in the form of pollution and noise, at least in the core area but potentially also in the more central sections of the 'fingers'.
Potential for social mix through variety of housing	Social mix could be reasonably good in the 'fingers', which offer the potential of a variety of dwelling forms, from multi-storey tenement accommodation in and around the primary and secondary cores to terraces and single-family housing at the edges of the 'fingers' towards the country; high land values in the core area may prevent social mix unless a proportion of housing were to be subsidised.
Potential for local autonomy	A degree of local autonomy may be possible in the 'fingers' where development may be less intense and more varied. As with the core city, the central area, with higher density and complexity, may have similar but less acute problems with community participation.
Potential for self-sufficiency	Self-sufficiency can be achieved as a result of the inclusion of open land between the 'fingers'. The open land is fragmented but the areas between the 'fingers' are still of considerable continuity.
Degree of adaptability	Expansion is largely limited to the 'fingers', but growth increases distances to the city centre and the rigid geometry prevents major organisational changes. At the micro-scale adaptability is possible only by replacement.
Imageability of the city (the physical entity) as a whole	The imageability of the star city as an entity is good only as long as the star remains relatively small. With growing size and population the overall expansion of the city may prevent any imageability of the city as an entity.
Imageability of parts of the city (neighbourhoods, districts, towns)	The central area should be readily imageable as a result of density and concentration of activities; the nodes around transport stops in the 'fingers' too may be imageable but need careful design attention.
Sense of place and centrality	The availability of a centre and subcentres in the 'fingers' should generate a good sense of place and centrality as long as these places are well designed and have clearly distinguishable features and sets of activities.

Table 3–04. *Evaluation of the performance of city models based on agreed sustainability characteristics: satellite city*

Characteristics	Performance of city model
Degree of containment of development	The overall city or metropolis is a cluster of towns, each potentially as compact as the core city but of limited size and spatially separated from each other. Like the star city model, the satellite city incorporates open land, in this model around the central city and the satellites, and accordingly the urban fabric is fragmented.
Population density relative to land needed	The gross population density is similar or equal to that of other city models. As in the star city, population is 'decentralised', but in this city model into separate towns rather than 'fingers'. In terms of population the central city may be somewhat larger than the satellites, but there will be hardly any variation of densities between the satellites and the central city; there may, however, be a variety of densities in each of them, from very high at the central nodes to medium at the borders with the countryside.
Viability of public transport	A primary public transport system will be viable as connector of the satellites with the central city, but also of the satellites with each other; the need to travel might be somewhat reduced by the fact that each cluster is to a high degree self-sufficient in terms of urban functions. Inside the compact towns public transport is essential to avoid car dependency, and both primary and secondary systems may be viable owing to the high concentration of population; there might, however, be a danger of congestion in the central areas of the towns.
Dispersal of vehicular traffic	Primary vehicular transport is likely to be concentrated into major channels linking the towns but, owing to the overall decentralisation, traffic should be dispersed and congestion avoided except in the core areas of the central city and satellites where restriction of vehicular traffic may be essential. As a result of the compactness of the central city and satellites, secondary vehicular traffic routes should be traffic-calmed.
Viability of mixed uses	There will be a considerable potential of mixed uses in the central city and the satellites owing to the decentralised concentration of the urban fabric.
Access to services and facilities	Access to central facilities in the core city and the satellites will be good as long as each satellite provides all the services and facilities required to make them largely independent from the central city; owing to the limitation of size, distances to the central core will be relatively small. The central city is likely to accommodate additional city-wide activities over and above those provided by the centres of the satellites.
Access to green open spaces (parks, countryside)	With limited size of the central city and the satellites the relationship with nature will be good as all entities are surrounded by open countryside; a symbiotic relationship with nature is therefore easily established. Access to open land is, however, somewhat uneven for central and edge locations in the central city and the satellites. The land itself is continuous as it flows around the towns.
Environmental conditions (noise, pollution, congestion)	Despite the compactness of the central city and the satellites, environmental conditions are likely to be good as a result of the fragmentation of the urban fabric and the limitation of the size and population in each of the towns; but there will be differences between central and edge locations in the towns.
Potential for social mix through variety of housing	There will be a limited potential for social mix in the central city and the satellites owing to their compactness and concentration of population; a range of different dwelling forms – from high-density low-rise in the central areas to family houses at the edge – may be provided but social housing may need to be heavily subsidised.
Potential for local autonomy	In comparison to the core city, the fragmentation of the urban fabric into smaller clusters should make it somewhat easier for communities to shape their own environment and become locally autonomous as long as the micro-structure of the clusters shows some form of hierarchy and as long as the towns are of small size. However, with continuous and unstructured development and with larger scale of the towns autonomy would be difficult to achieve.
Potential for self-sufficiency	Self-sufficiency can be achieved as a result of the inclusion of open land around the central city and satellites. The open land is somewhat fragmented but continuous.
Degree of adaptability	As long as growth is dealt with by multiplication rather than expansion of clusters the degree of the adaptation of the overall structure is high; however, stringent control would be required to prevent clusters and specifically the central city from growing beyond their optimum size. Inside each town adaptation is possible only by replacement.
Imageability of the city (the physical entity) as a whole	Imageability of the central city and the satellites is potentially very good, especially if each of them develops different forms in response to different local conditions and provided the size of the towns is limited.
Imageability of parts of the city (neighbourhoods, districts, towns)	Owing to the compactness of the urban fabric individual districts and neighbourhoods may not easily be distinguishable and require careful design and specific sets of activities to make them imageable.
Sense of place and centrality	The fact that each of the towns has a centre should generate a very good sense of place and centrality as long as the central places are well designed and have clearly distinguishable features and sets of activities.

Table 3–05. *Evaluation of the performance of city models based on agreed sustainability characteristics: galaxy of settlements (transit-oriented developments, traditional neighbourhood developments)*

Characteristics	Performance of city model
Degree of containment of development	Compactness can be achieved in the settlements or neighbourhoods, especially around the core and transport node, but containment of the urban fabric is poor owing to its fragmentation of the urban fabric into small development clusters. All settlements are surrounded by open land and spatially separated from one another.
Population density relative to land needed	The gross population density is similar or equal to that of the other city models, but population is dispersed to an even greater degree than in the star and satellite city into small groups of between 3,000 and 6,000 people. There will be hardly any variation of density between individual settlements, but there may be a variety of densities within each of them, from high at the central node to low at the border with the countryside.
Viability of public transport	A primary public transport system would not be viable unless the settlements clustered along existing routes between core cities. A secondary public transport system can be expected to be even less viable, owing to the relatively small population targeted at each node.
Dispersal of vehicular traffic	As the population is highly dispersed into small pockets of development, the car can be expected to be the main means of transport; vehicular traffic would, however, be dispersed on a large number of roads, and there would be no serious problem with congestion anywhere in the galaxy.
Viability of mixed uses	Mixed use in any of the settlements would be viable only to a limited degree, owing to the limited number of people supporting services and facilities.
Access to services and facilities	Access to local services and facilities at the centres of each settlement would be within walking and cycling distance, but provision would be for daily or weekly needs only. For access to any other services and facilities the settlements would rely on a core city and accessibility can be expected to be poor.
Access to green open spaces (parks, countryside)	The relationship of the neighbourhoods with nature would be good and access to the country would be within walking and cycling distance. The open land would, however, be highly fragmented and this would reduce scale and flexibility of use.
Environmental conditions (noise, pollution, congestion)	Owing to the limited size of settlements and the availability of open land around all of them environmental conditions would be very good throughout.
Potential for social mix through variety of housing	The limited size of settlements favours the provision of a large variety of different dwelling forms; the potential for social mix would accordingly be high.
Potential for local autonomy	Owing to the limited population and size of settlements communities would have an excellent opportunity to shape and actually build their own environment.
Potential for self-sufficiency	Self-sufficiency can be achieved as the result of the availability of open land around the settlements but the land is highly fragmented and might be unsuitable for larger-scale uses such as industry, forestry, farming.
Degree of adaptability	Overall the galaxy can expand by multiplication of settlements. As a result of the high fragmentation of the urban fabric flexibility of change would, however, be minimal and adaptation would be by replacement only.
Imageability of the city (the physical entity) as a whole	Overall the imageability of the galaxy would be non-existent as the urban fabric is highly dispersed and as there is no central focus.
Imageability of parts of the city (neighbourhoods, districts, towns)	The nodes within the settlements would allow some limited imageability but the settlements may be hardly distinguishable from one another unless central nodes have clearly distinguishable features.
Sense of place and centrality	The nodes at the centres of settlements may provide some local sense of place and centrality, but overall there are no major focal points, owing to the lack of a hierarchy of centres.

Table 3–06. Evaluation of the performance of city models based on agreed sustainability characteristics: linear city

Characteristics	Performance of city model
Degree of containment of development	Compactness can be achieved in the band of linear development, specifically around transport nodes and the development area along the central transport line. However, the linear form of this city model will inevitably result in larger and larger distances between parts of the growing city; development is continuous but overall not compact.
Population density relative to land needed	The gross population density is potentially similar or equal to that of other city models, but owing to the shallow though continuous nature of the city form, population is stretched out along the linear transport route. There will hardly be any variation of population density between different areas of this city model, but there may be a variety of densities from high at transport nodes and along the central transport line to low at the edges of the city where it meets the countryside.
Viability of public transport	The entire structure is based on linear transportation and is conducive to a main public transport system that forms the spine of the city. A secondary transport system – required if the depth of the city is increased to reduce its overall length – might, however, be less viable, owing to the smaller population size targeted at each stretch of the linear city. If the main transit system is fast with long distances between stops, access is better from the areas around the stops and worse from development between these areas.
Dispersal of vehicular traffic	A major vehicular traffic route would run in parallel with the main linear public transport line, secondary traffic routes would lead to and away from the primary linear route. As population is stretched out there might be no great danger of serious congestion in areas on either side of and away from the linear spine, but in the spine itself some congestion may occur, owing to the inevitable concentration of traffic.
Viability of mixed uses	A concentration of services and facilities is possible in the central spine area of the linear city, specifically around transport nodes; but provision is likely to be for daily or weekly needs only, owing to the limited number of people in the nodes' catchment area; lacking, therefore, is a hierarchy of provision centres.
Access to services and facilities	With shallow development depth access to services and facilities and to public transport stops is within walking and cycling distance; however, only provision for daily or weekly needs is likely to be available. Provision above this level needs to be provided by core cities which the linear city may link; regarding services and facilities the linear city form is therefore not efficient on its own.
Access to green open spaces (parks, countryside)	The limited depth of development away from the central linear transport line allows good access to the surrounding countryside, within walking and cycling distance. There are shorter and longer distances to the country depending on the location in the linear development band, but generally access can be expected to be reasonably even for almost all areas of the city. The country itself is continuous.
Environmental conditions (noise, pollution, congestion)	Owing to the shallow depth of the linear city environmental conditions are likely to be very good overall though there may be some variation between conditions in central spine and edge locations.
Potential for social mix through variety of housing	There is potential for a variety of different dwelling types from high-density low-rise around nodes and along the central spine to family homes at the borders with the countryside; the potential for social mix is therefore good.
Potential for local autonomy	The potential for local autonomy depends upon the micro-structure of this city model. It might be difficult to establish autonomous areas as the urban fabric develops continuously unless there is a clear organisation of districts and neighbourhoods with their cores. A hierarchical differentiation between districts and towns is likely to be lacking.
Potential for self-sufficiency	The close relationship with the countryside would enable a symbiotic relationship between city and uninterrupted country and a high degree of self-sufficiency could be achieved.
Degree of adaptability	The structure is extendible on either end but the overall form and structure of the city is dictated by one main circulation route and therefore rigid. Local changes would be possible by replacement only.
Imageability of the city (the physical entity) as a whole	The considerable length of this city model prevents imageability of the city as an entity.
Imageability of parts of the city (neighbourhoods, districts, towns)	The imageability of parts depends on the micro-structure of this city model and may not be all that good as a result of continuous development unless the transport and provision nodes are carefully designed and differentiated.
Sense of place and centrality	With continuous linear development there is a lack of centrality which might be psychologically problematic; some sense of place may, however, develop around transport nodes.

Table 3–07. Evaluation of the performance of city models based on agreed sustainability characteristics: polycentric net or regional city

Characteristics	Performance of city model
Degree of containment of development	Compactness can be achieved in nodal and linear development areas but – like the star, the combination of stars and the satellite city model – the regional city incorporates open land within its structure and accordingly the urban fabric is fragmented.
Population density relative to land needed	The gross population density is similar or equal to that of other city models, but the regional city is likely to incorporate a number of different development clusters with different sizes and populations and to provide a variety of more or less densely grouped areas. There may also be a variety of densities from very high at centres of larger clusters (towns or cities) to medium or even low at smaller and more fragmented areas.
Viability of public transport	Structure and form of the polycentric net are the result of a network of public transport lines with primary and secondary systems meeting at a multiplicity of different centres of different size, capacity and specialisation. All primary and secondary transport systems in the larger development areas can be expected to be viable. In the smaller and more fragmented areas, only the secondary transport system may be feasible, and less viable owing to the fragmentation of population.
Dispersal of vehicular traffic	Vehicular traffic would generally be dispersed except where converging on larger centres, where congestion is likely to occur. Roads inside higher-density development areas should therefore be traffic-calmed to avoid environmental and functional problems; major vehicular traffic routes should be outside or in between development areas.
Viability of mixed uses	Owing to the potential for the forming of a multiplicity of hierarchically differentiated centres the potential for mixed use is good but variable. The larger development areas will accommodate more intense and more city-wide activities and therefore a large variety of different uses; the smaller development clusters may have provisions for daily or weekly needs only and therefore accommodate a smaller number of different uses.
Access to services and facilities	Access to provision centres should generally be good but can be expected to be uneven; a hierarchy of public transport systems will, however, provide the required mobility for inhabitants to have considerable choice between centres of provision of different size, capacity and specialisation.
Access to green open spaces (parks, countryside)	The fragmentation of the urban fabric and the incorporation of open land will allow good but (with varying distances from centres of larger or smaller development areas) uneven access to green spaces. Some of the open land may be trapped between development, which would reduce its environmental impact and usability; other green spaces may be continuously linked to the country; but overall a symbiotic relationship with nature could be established.
Environmental conditions (noise, pollution, congestion)	Environmental conditions should be good overall but they are likely to be uneven as a result of larger or smaller development areas, of more or less continuous development in parts of the regional city. Higher concentration of development may cause some noise, pollution and congestion problems; in smaller and/or more isolated development areas environmental conditions will be very good.
Potential for social mix through variety of housing	There is good potential for social mix as a result of the diversity of development clusters, but it is likely that there will be differences between larger development areas with higher densities at their centre (less potential for a variety of forms of habitation and social mix) and smaller development areas with lower densities (more potential for a variety of forms of habitation and social mix).
Potential for local autonomy	The potential for local autonomy is good in the smaller development areas and in those larger areas which have a clear hierarchical structure of areas and nodes.
Potential for self-sufficiency	The overall potential for self-sufficiency is as high as for the other city types, but within the different areas of the regional city there will be better and worse access to more continuous and more fragmented open land with various degrees of usability of the land.
Degree of adaptability	The entire structure of the regional city is open-ended and adaptable as it has no rigid geometry and can grow and shrink at macro-scale; changes at micro-scale are expected to be by replacement only.
Imageability of the city (the physical entity) as a whole	The potentially limitless size of the regional city prevents imageability of the city as an entity.
Imageability of parts of the city (neighbourhoods, districts, towns)	Nodes and transport channels can be expected to have a strong visual image provided they, and the areas they serve, have distinguishable design features and sets of activities.
Sense of place and centrality	The multiplicity of different nodes at the centres of different urban areas should provide a strong sense of place and a sense of centrality at different hierarchical levels.

Table 3–08. *Comparison of the expected performance of the six city models*

Criteria	Core city	star city	Sat. city	TODs, TNDs	Lin. city	Reg. city
Degree of containment of development	+	+/−	+/−	−	−	+/−
Population density relative to land needed	+	+/−	+	+	+	+
Viability of public transport	+	+/−	+	−	+	+
Dispersal of vehicular transport	−	+/−	+/−	+	−	+/−
Viability of mixed uses	+	+/−	+	−	+/−	+/−
Access to services and facilities	+/−	+/−	+/−	−	+/−	+/−
Access to green open spaces (parks, countryside)	−	+	+	+	+	+
Environmental conditions (noise, pollution, congestion)	−	+/−	+/−	+	+	+/−
Potential for social mix through variety of housing	−	+/−	+/−	+	+/−	+/−
Potential for local autonomy	−	+/−	+/−	+	+/−	+/−
Potential for self-sufficiency	+	+	+	+	+	+
Degree of adaptability of city to changing conditions/needs	−	+/−	+/−	−	+/−	+
Imageability of the city (the physical entity) as a whole	+/−	+/−	+/−	−	−	+/−
Imageability of parts of the city (neighbourhoods, districts, towns)	+/−	+/−	+/−	+	+/−	+/−
Sense of place and centrality	+/−	+/−	+	−	−	+
Equal weights	−1	+2	+6	+1	+1	+6
Weighted (bold)	−4	+1	+2	0	0	+3

Note: Sat. = satellite; TOD = transit-oriented development; TND = traditional neighbourhood development; lin. = linear; reg. = regional

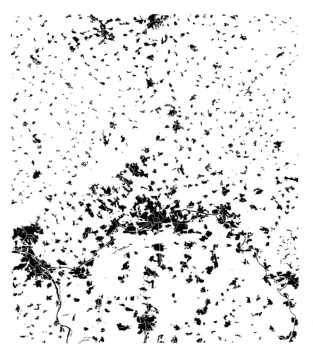

3–29. *Figure-ground of the Rhine–Main region in Germany (Magistrat der Stadt Frankfurt am Main, 1995; reproduced by kind permission of the Magistrate of the city of Frankfurt am Main)*

3.5 Viability of the Models in Terms of the Required Changes to the Urban Fabric of Existing Cities

Comparison so far indicates that a decentralised city form may achieve the same values in terms of total area, population density, overall dimensions, provision of open land, etc. as the core city, but may provide a better environment and easier access to the country. These advantages become especially clear as the city's population grows: at 500,000 a decentralised city form seems to become preferable; the core city performs best when relatively small, with a population of up to 250,000.

Over and above the criteria applied in this evaluation, there is one other important issue that needs to be taken into consideration. If the viability of the transformation of our existing cities, dispersed as almost all of them are *(Fig. 3.29)*, into any of the above models were to be considered, the core city would most likely lose out because it would require the largest degree of rearrangement of urban fabric. The strongly geometric models, the star and linear city, would perhaps also require a high degree of rearrangement of urban fabric as long as these city models remained isolated events. In comparison, the regional city model, i.e. a composite city form, perhaps as a combination of smaller core, star, satellite and linear cities, can take on practically any configuration and can respond to local conditions. It would therefore seem to be the most appropriate urban model, potentially with the lowest degree of rearrangement required.

3.6 A City Form Based on Transport Systems

The inclusion of a variety of functional, social, economic and environmental criteria in the evaluation of urban models of different forms and structures strengthens the argument for a composite city form. In view of the rather poor performance of the core city in some aspects, one cannot help forming the impression that the search for one generally valid form of sustainable city, e.g. the compact city, might be in vain and perhaps a little naive. Furthermore, knowing that the major task is not the design of a new and 'ideal' city but the redesign of existing cities, one needs to take into consideration that each existing city is unique in its physical structure and form, land-use pattern, activities, socio-economic conditions, history, topography and micro-climate and so on, and there may simply *have* to be different planning and design approaches for different cities in order for them to become more sustainable. But to return to the comparison of city models, there is another issue which greatly influences city form; it has already been touched upon but needs further exploration.

Walking as an alternative means of transport provides access to services and facilities as long as these are located within 10 minutes' walk from one's front door. Because of the limited population that can live within a 600 m radius, local facilities can be expected to provide only for the most essential daily needs. Mobility over and above walking distance is therefore essential for today's urban society, which relies on ever more specific uses and specialised provisions which do not necessarily depend on central locations (see Farthing *et al.*, 1996, p. 182; Breheny, 1992, pp. 138–59). Recreational facilities or workplaces, for example, are provided in increasing varieties and in a large number of different locations. Access to these locations offers a choice of different qualities and types of services and facilities in the city. Transport is therefore of the utmost importance for the quality of urban life. City forms that facilitate transport, specifically those that support public transport, are therefore more appropriate than city forms that do not. One may therefore conclude that, in terms of mobility and transport, the most efficient city form is the one that follows the transport network, but not all forms of transport networks are equally efficient.

The star, the linear and the regional city develop along transport routes. In the star formation the routes converge at a central point, the city centre. Experience with city development in the past shows that with growing size of the city the more central stretches of the transport lines will become more and more congested as long as the city relies on one single core. The polycentric net does not have converging traffic routes in a single core but, like Calthorpe's TODs along a network of 'trunk lines and feeder bus routes' (Calthorpe, 1993,

p. 62), a number of lines crossing at a number of nodes. In this configuration transport is dispersed rather than concentrated, enabling reasonably equal access to all urban areas, and the danger of traffic congestion is relatively small as long as none of the nodes at a transport interchange grows too large. This means that a transport network will work best if it does not rely on a single core, i.e. if the city is multi-nucleated.

The replacement of the radial and circumferential network of transport in the traditional city by a pattern based on a large-scale gridiron plan was suggested by traffic engineers and planners in the early 1960s because the grid serves all areas of a city or metropolitan area rather than a single point at the core of a traditional centralised city (Fisher, 1962, p. 58). At a time when in Glasgow the transport planners established a radial and circumferential transport structure for a city which actually grew more linearly than radially, city planners elsewhere had already recognised that such a structure will eventually lead to congestion in the core and inner ring area (Manners, 1970, pp. 232-4). The Chicago Area Transportation Plan of 1962, for instance, shows the old radial and circumferential transport network to be expanded into, and to a degree superseded by, a grid pattern (Chicago Area Transportation Plan, 1992, p. 112). By now the fact that ring roads do not solve traffic problems but create more problems is a daily experience in many cities.

Development along public transport lines, and specifically at transport stops, allows easy access to public transport systems as long as development is shallow, i.e. not more than 600 m away from public transport lines and stops. This leads to an urban structure with high-density mixed-use cores of development forming primary centres at crossing points of a public transport grid; high-density mixed-use nodes of development at transport stops of a single line form secondary centres. This structure seems identical with Calthorpe's pattern of TODs, except that the primary and secondary centres can be expected to be much larger than neighbourhoods and

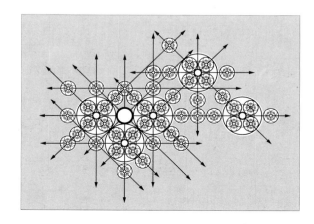

3–30. *The regional city with transport grid, primary and secondary centres*

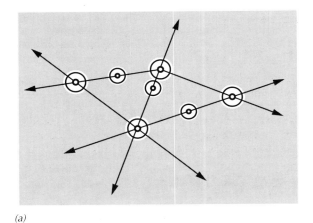

(a)

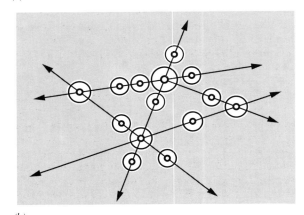

(b)

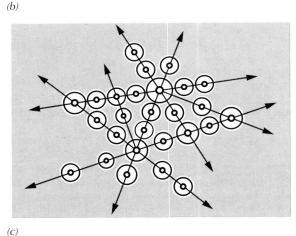

(c)

3–31. *Different degrees of compactness of the regional city*

that access to a hierarchy of centres is provided by a hierarchy of public transport *(Fig. 3.30)*.

Without going into the micro-scale structure of components of the city, I still need to discuss the 'calibration' of the net, not in terms of densities but in terms of the distances between lines of different transport systems, which will undoubtedly influence their accessibility on

the one hand and their viability on the other. Regarding densities, the city model comparison has shown that fragmentation of urban fabric may not necessarily generate low overall population densities as long as the most compact of city models, the core city, also includes a certain amount of open land, which it requires for social, environmental and ecological reasons. A polycentric net, therefore, may not necessarily have to be unconfined, of low density and loosely structured; in places it may actually be rather compact, in other places less so, depending on the amount of open land integrated into the structure. The net may be loosely structured, with larger distances between development components such as core 'villages' or core 'towns', i.e. with a larger proportion of agricultural and forestry land, in more rural and country town areas, and it may be more compact, i.e. include less open land, in city and metropolitan areas *(Fig. 3.31)*. Even the structure of a large city or metropolitan area may form a more compact net in some parts, e.g. in its central area, and a less compact net in others, e.g. at its edges.

3.7 What is Achieved by the Net City Model

References to historical city structures clearly indicate that the composite or 'net' city model is not a new invention. There have been primary and secondary centres at the heart of the medieval or traditional town and its districts or neighbourhoods (Krier's *quartiers*; Krier, 1984, pp. 70–1). What is added to this structure is the notion of continuity over entire metropolitan areas and the inclusion of open countryside within the structure – but this too is not new and was successfully demonstrated by Ebenezer Howard a hundred years ago. However, the combination of a hierarchical micro-structure of neighbourhoods, districts and towns and an integrating transport macro-structure allowing the parts of the micro-structure to form urban regions seems to offer for the regeneration of existing cities a more flexible and, it is hoped, a more readily applicable model of a more sustainable city than Howard's 'city cluster'. The net may consist not of equal 'cities' but of a combination of independent neighbourhoods or villages, districts or *quartiers*, towns and cities which may be more or less densely integrated, more rural or more urban, depending on the amount of land included in between the individual elements of the net and the resulting distances between them. The net is also not a combination of entities which remain static, at least in dimension and population, once they have reached their maximum size, but a dynamic system that may change by the growing and shrinking of its parts as long as this process is based on the same micro-structure, which generates a variety of meaningful places regardless of the size of a conurbation, and on the same macro-structure, which links all semi-autonomous parts.

What is achieved by the net city model in terms of sustainability is potentially considerable:

- In formal and spatial terms the individual elements of the net, be they neighbourhood, district or town, may be clearly identifiable and highly imageable as semi-autonomous places with their own design characteristics and patterns of use. Each of these elements – which may be clearly identifiable as entities (because they are separated out like Venice's neighbourhoods) or more integrated (because they overlap like Florence's neighbourhoods) – may provide a sense of place and a focus for a sense of belonging for its inhabitants.

- In socio-economic terms the formation of identifiable spatial and social entities may provide a better chance of social mix, achieved through a variety of different house and tenure forms, and a variety of different uses, both of which would be encouraged through the large variety of different semi-autonomous places. The decentralisation of some of the central city functions into town and district cores (if not neighbourhood centres) is likely to achieve a mixture of uses and a high degree of interaction with and access for communities. The management of open countryside as part of the net city is likely to generate workplaces and the opportunity for entrepreneurial activities for city farms, forests, food production, recreation and sports, which could benefit the city's entities as well as the city at large. The hierarchical micro-structure would also enable communities to become actively involved in the shaping and management of their urban areas and would help achieve a degree of autonomy as long as the power of decision-making is decentralised.

- In environmental and ecological terms the inclusion of open countryside in the city structure, ideally open linear wedges linking directly and without interruption to the natural environment, would enable the building up of a symbiotic relationship between city and countryside.

- In functional terms the net city model would allow the formation of small and large conglomerations of settlements of more rural or more urban character by applying the same principles of hierarchical and network structure. The ability to respond to changing conditions and requirements is high and, owing to its flexibility, the structure is likely to be adaptable to most local conditions and applicable in many if not most already partially decentralised cities and metropolitan areas.

3.8 Conclusions

The investigation of city forms that respond positively to the generally agreed upon sustainability criteria has come up with evidence that both the micro- and the macro-structure of the city are of considerable importance. The first provides access to services and facilities and to transport nodes, and therefore responds to the most basic functional needs of provision and mobility. The second influences the environmental quality of urban areas and access to open spaces and the country-side, and with it the potential for a symbiotic relation-ship between city and country.

It has become clear that a hierarchical structure of provision centres and transport systems and nodes is valid for all cities, city regions and conurbations. It has also become clear that cities and conurbations can have a variety of different macro-structures as long as they have the appropriate micro-structure of nodes and link-ages that is responsible for access to provisions and ser-vices and mobility.

All conclusions regarding micro- and macro-structure represent highly probable assumptions, some of which are based on empirical data to back them up (or, indeed, to refute them). A virtual (or, better, a real city) laboratory would be most useful in order to obtain additional evidence and empirical data. Many attempts have been made to obtain research grants in order to establish such a laboratory, but to date they have failed; the bodies that provide grants seem to be content with clearly defined and rather limited (and therefore inevitably exclusive) research proposals and do not seem to understand the need for multi-aspect and multi-disciplinary research, which they consider to be too complex and ambitious to be successful. Well, much of current research in the field of the 'sustainable city', for all its mostly inconclusive results, demonstrates that without ambition the complex issues of a sustainable city region will not become more tangible and we will continue to rely on assumptions.

What can, however, be done in this context is to pro-vide evidence that the developed micro- and macro-structures are relevant for real cities and city regions and can be applied in an attempt to generate a better-functioning and more user- and environment-friendly city. Therefore in Chapter 5 an attempt is made to explore the applicability of the model urban structure developed as a result of the comparison of the performance of dif-ferent city forms and the pursuit of sustainability parame-ters. Glasgow will be used as exemplar and the objective will be to find out how, and to what degree, the applica-tion of the net city model could be viable.

References

Abercrombie, p. (1945) *Greater London Plan 1944*, HMSO, London.

Alexander, C. (1988) A city is not a tree, in Thackara, J. (ed.) *Design after Modernism*, Thames and Hudson, London.

Alexander, C., Ishikawa, S. and Silverstein, M. (1975) *A Pattern Language: Towns, Buildings, Construction*, Oxford University Press, New York.

Bacon, E. (1992) *Design of Cities*, Thames and Hudson, London.

Blumenfeld, H. (1949) Theory of city form, past and present, *Journal of the Society of Architectural Historians*, 8, pp. 7–16.

Breheny, M.J. (1992) The contradictions of the compact city, in Breheny, M.J. (ed.) *Sustainable Development and Urban Form*, Pion, London.

Breheny, M.J. (1996) Centrists, decentrists and compromisers, in Jenks, M., Burton, E. and Williams, K. (eds) *The Compact City: A Sustainable Urban Form?* E & FN Spon, London.

Calthorpe, P. (1993) *The Next American Metropolis: Ecology, Community and the American Dream*, Princeton Architectural Press, New York.

Chicago Area Transportation Study (1992) *Final Report*, Vol. III, Transportation Plan, Chicago.

Christaller, W. (1933) *Die zentralen Orte in Süddeutschland*, Gustav Fischer, Jena.

Ciuffini, F.M. (1995) *The Sustainable City – A European Tetralogy, Part III: Transport and Public Spaces: The Connective Tissue of the Sustainable City*, European Foundation for the Improvement of Living and Working Conditions, Dublin.

Department of the Environment (1993) *Planning Policy Guidance 6: Town Centres and Retail Developments*, HMSO, London.

Department of the Environment and Department of Transport (1994) *Planning Policy Guidance 13: Transport*, HMSO, London.

Duany, A. and Plater-Zyberk, E. (1991) *Towns and Town Making Principles*, Harvard University Graduate School of Design/Rizzoli, New York.

Farthing, S., Winter, J. and Coombes, T. (1996) Travel behaviour and local accessibility of services and facilities, in Jenks, M., Burton, E. and Williams, K. (eds) *The Compact City: A Sustainable Urban Form?* E & FN Spon, London.

Fisher, H.T. (1962) Radials and circumferentials: an outmoded urban concept?, in Williams, T.E.H. (ed.) *Urban Survival and Traffic*, E & FN Spon, London.

Geddes, P. (1915) *Cities in Evolution*, Williams & Norgate, London.

Glasgow City Council (1995) *Ward Profiles*, City Planning Department, Glasgow.

Hall, P. (1990) *Cities of Tomorrow*, Basil Blackwell, Oxford.

Hartoft-Nielson, P. (1993) The Danish experience: Copenhagen, in *The European City and Its Region: How Can the Co-ordination of Physical Planning Be Achieved?* International conference, Dublin, October 1993, organised by the Department of the Environment, Ireland, in conjunction with the Directorate-General for Regional Policies of the European Commission.

Hillman, M. (1996) In favour of the compact city, in Jenks, M., Burton, E. and Williams, K. (eds) *The Compact City: A Sustainable Urban Form?* E & FN Spon, London.

Howard, E. (1898) *To-morrow: A Peaceful Path to Real Reform*, Swan Sonnenshein, London. (Later republished as *Garden Cities of Tomorrow*)

Koetter, F. (1992) USA experience. *Urban Design Quarterly*, 42, pp. 17–21.

Krier, L. (1984) Houses, palaces, cities, in Papadakis, A. (ed.) *Architectural Design* Profile 54.

Kurokawa, K. (1987) New Tokyo plan, 2025. *The Japan Architect*, 367/368, Nov/Dec, pp. 46–63.

Lawrence, G. (1996) The Seattle approach. *Urban Design Quarterly*, 57, pp. 23–5.

Lynch, K. (1961 [1991]) The pattern of the metropolis, in Banarjee, T. and Southworth, M. (eds) (1991) *City Sense and City Design: Writings and Projects of Kevin Lynch*, MIT Press, Cambridge, Mass., pp. 47–64.

Lynch, K. (1985) *Good City Form*, MIT Press, Cambridge, Mass.

Lynch, K. (1986) *The Image of the City*, MIT Press, Cambridge, Mass.

Magistrat der Stadt Frankfurt am Main, Dezernat Planung, Amt für kommunale Gesamtentwicklung (1995) *Bericht zur Stadtentwicklung Frankfurt am Main 1995*, Frankfurt.

Manners, G. (1970) Urban expansion in the United States, in Leahy, W.H., McKee, D.L. and Dean, R.D. (eds) *Urban Economics: Theory, Development and Planning*, The Free Press, New York.

Ministry of Housing, Physical Planning and the Environment (1991) *Fourth Report (EXTRA) on Physical Planning in the Netherlands: On the Road to 2015,* The Hague.

Minnery, J.R. (1992) *Urban Form and Development Strategies: Equity, Environmental and Economic Implications,* Centre for Urban and Regional Development, Queensland University of Technology, Queensland (for the National Housing Strategy).

Moughtin, C. (1996) *Urban Design: Green Dimensions,* Butterworth Architecture, Oxford.

Mumford, L. (1984) *The City in History,* Penguin Books, Harmondsworth.

Scoffham, E. and Vale, B. (1996) How compact is sustainable – how sustainable is compact?, in Jenks, M., Burton, E. and Williams, K. (eds) *The Compact City: A Sustainable Urban Form?* E & FN Spon, London.

Stretton, H. (1971) *Ideas for Australian Cities,* Georgian House, Melbourne.

Thomas, L. and Cousins, W. (1996) The compact city: a successful, desirable and achievable urban form?, in Jenks, M., Burton, E. and Williams, K. (eds) *The Compact City: A Sustainable Urban Form?* E & FN Spon, London.

Urban Villages Group (1992) *Urban Villages,* Urban Villages Group, London.

van der Valk, A. and Faludi, A. (1992) Growth regions and the future of Dutch planning doctrine, in Breheny, M.J. (ed.) *Sustainable Development and Urban Form,* Pion, London.

Williams, K., Burton, E. and Jenks, M. (1996) Achieving the compact city through intensification, in Jenks, M., Burton, E. and Williams, K. (eds) *The Compact City: A Sustainable Urban Form?* E & FN Spon, London.

Part Two

Application of the Model Urban Structure to Glasgow

Glasgow: A Typical Post-industrial City

4

As explained in Chapter 3, the focus of this book is urban design on the city-region/city and city district level. The aim is to illustrate the contribution strategic urban design can and should make to the improvement of the form and structure of today's city. A generally valid micro-structure has been defined and a number of macro-structures have been compared. It is now important to illustrate their applicability in and validity for an existing urban area and the one chosen for this purpose is the city region of Glasgow.

The reasons for this choice are simple. Glasgow is a city which clearly demonstrates all the symptoms of dispersal, car dependency and social stratification so typical for many post-industrial cities in Europe. But it is also a city which exemplifies great strength in its historical development, and a high degree of spatial and formal cohesion in those areas of the city centre and some inner suburbs which have escaped comprehensive redevelopment. Glasgow is therefore a good city with which to experiment with strategic urban design interventions.

The aim of such interventions and restructuring proposals in and for Glasgow is not to put forward workable solutions to the city's problems, though the developed design frameworks, if adopted, in part if not in total, might well help achieve a better city. The interventions are to be understood as exemplification of arguments and strategic design approaches with the help of which one might achieve a better-functioning, less socially stratified and more people-friendly and less congested city.

Of course, when applying strategic design frameworks in Glasgow, the illustrated interventions are inevitably place-specific; they have to respond to the specific characteristics of this city and its past and recent history. The design approaches and principles employed are nevertheless believed to be generally applicable, though they would achieve divergent results in different cities owing to the changed characteristics and conditions.

It cannot be expected that all readers are sufficiently familiar with Glasgow, its urban form and structure, to follow easily the arguments and proposed frameworks generated in the subsequent sections. This chapter therefore provides a very short description of the major characteristics of this city and provides some explanations as to how it developed into what it is, without going deeply into the city's history, which is well covered by other publications (specifically Reed, 1993). This introduction provides an opportunity to reflect not only upon development principles and patterns but also upon the role of planning and design in the main development periods of the city.

4.1 Glasgow's Development up to the Inter-war Period

At the end of the First World War Glasgow had long reached and already passed the height of its industrial development but – with the exception of the intrusion of nineteenth-century railways, which in the twentieth century would be paralleled by the intrusion of motorways – had not yet undergone any major changes regarding its development patterns, which are all based on traditional principles shared by many industrial cities throughout Europe. At this stage one would therefore expect the most coherent city form and structure, if such coherence ever existed.

The Major Characteristics of the Industrial City

Regarding the development pattern of the city at large, the Ordnance Survey (OS) map of 1915/16 shows a fairly dense and compact development in the central area of the city on both sides of the River Clyde (Fig. 4.01a). But development has already started to branch out to the north (Possilpark and Springburn), to the east (Calton, Bridgeton/Dalmarnock and Parkhead), to the south across an east–west railway line (Pollokshields/Govanhill immediately south of the railway line; further south, beyond Queens Park, Pollokshaws, Shawlands, Langside, Battlefield and Mount Florida), to the west (Govan south of the Clyde; Whiteinch/Broomhill and Partick and the West End north of the Clyde), to the north-west (Maryhill).

However, despite the development of suburbs, the city overall is still fairly compact; in 1912 it occupies only 44.8% of today's city area (today's political boundaries excluding Rutherglen) *(Fig. 4.01b)*. According to *Factsheet 2* (Glasgow City Council, 1997/98), the total area of Glasgow in 1912 was 7,763 ha, and the esti-

mated population for the same year was around 871,700 (an accurate figure is not available, but an approximate figure has been interpolated from information on the population growth); the gross population density in the city was accordingly around 110 persons per hectare (pph), equivalent to some of the highest densities in the historical areas of the city today.

Closer inspection of the OS map *(Fig. 4.01a)* shows that these suburban areas developing away from the central area are spatially separated by railway lines (particularly to the south and between the centre and Springburn to the north), the River Kelvin and Kelvin-

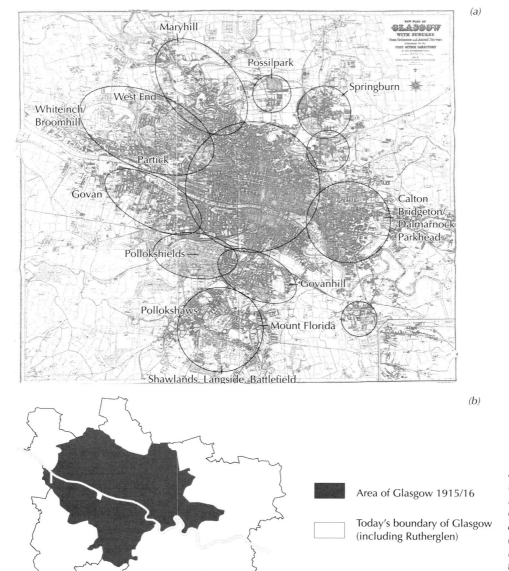

(a)

(b)

■ Area of Glasgow 1915/16

□ Today's boundary of Glasgow (including Rutherglen)

4–01. The extent of Glasgow's development in 1915/16: (a) Ordnance Survey map of Glasgow, 1915/16; (b) the area of Glasgow in 1915/16 inside today's city boundaries (based on Glasgow City Council, 1997/98 Factsheet 1)

grove Park (separating the West End from the central area), and a combination of parks and railway area east of the centre (from the Necropolis/Cathedral area via College Goods Yard to Glasgow Green and Richmond Park). Along the railway lines and the River Clyde intense industrial activities were accommodated which reinforce the barrier between the central and the suburban areas of the city. These barriers have influenced much of the subsequent development of Glasgow and are still present today *(Fig. 4.02)*.

Though development in the central area can be seen to be continuous, in land-use terms there is no clear city core which accommodates all city-wide activities. Glasgow has no concentric structure with a clearly defined core and rings of development surrounding it. From its origins at High Street and Trongate/Gallowgate the city grew on either side of the River Clyde roughly to the east and west, occupying a broad band of terrain running generally from north-west to south-east, with a lower terrace of a width of between 1.6 and 2.4 km, an area under water in Neolithic times *(Fig. 4.03)*, and a high terrace on either side bounded to the south-west and north-east by hills.

In the centre of this terrain is a strip of development north of the river, roughly between the origin of the city and the West End, accommodating a mixture of commerce, retail, education, housing, cultural institutions, churches, university buildings and public administration. One would normally find many of those elements in the city core, but in Glasgow they are spread out over an area of approximately 4 km in length (in an east–west direction) and a depth (in a north–south direction) varying between about 1.5 and 2 km.

This central area is surrounded to the north, east and south by development clusters – suburbs, often nuclear in form around the cross of the burgh, but then further developed on the basis of shared principles of grid structure, perimeter block development, building typology – accommodating a mixture of light and heavy industry and high-density working-class tenements. Outside this U-shaped industrial and tenement area, mostly but not entirely to the west, are the outer suburbs for the middle classes, also adhering to similar development principles but grander in scale, design and landscaping.

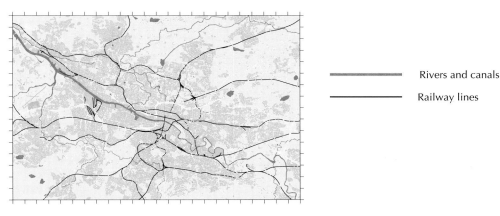

████████████ Rivers and canals

—————————— Railway lines

4–02. Glasgow's historical edges: railway lines, rivers and canals

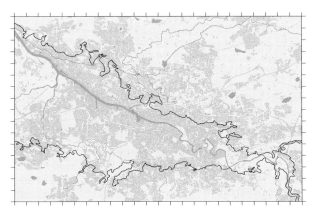

⌂ Edge of lower terrace (25 m contour line)

4–03. The Clyde valley: edge of the lower terrace (plan/diagram)

The Common Characteristics of Development Clusters

The 1915/16 Ordnance Survey map *(Fig. 4.01a)* also reveals astonishingly consistent development patterns in the city's different districts despite the fact that development was incremental, as a result of largely speculative projects of individual and generally local investors, without much of a formal planning process (see Reed, 1993, specifically chapters 2, 3 and 5). The design principles responsible for the consistency of the emerging patterns are:

- a more or less regular, open-ended and non-hierarchical grid pattern, so typical of Glasgow, which is modified in places in response to context conditions, for instance where medieval street crosses of former independent burghs are incorporated into the growing city, or as adaptation to topography, rivers and the like, or when specific building configurations are introduced that require the modification of the grid *(Fig. 4.04)*;

- the perimeter block development principle, which has been applied over centuries in almost all traditional cities; building mass, occasionally fragmented (in the few villa areas) but mostly continuous, is located along the outer edges of a development plot or city block, with building entrances more or less directly off the streets, providing the possibility of good interaction between people in public spaces and private buildings, with semi-private courtyards sheltered by the perimeter buildings from the public, and continuously enclosed streets and squares appearing as though they have been carved out of a solid mass *(Fig. 4.05)*;

- the repetition of a few standard building types such as the tenement, again so typical of Glasgow and other Scottish towns, the terrace, the urban villa, the multi-storey warehouse and office building, etc. *(Fig. 4.06 a–e)*;

- high-density development throughout, in the city centre up to seven or so storeys, in housing areas three or four storeys, whether the house type is a working-class tenement or a middle-class West End terrace or West End tenement (compare the typology);

- horizontal, and in shopping streets frequently vertical, mixture of uses *(Fig. 4.07)*, with living accommodation next to commercial and industrial uses and above shops.

Many of these characteristics are shared by a multitude of traditional cities. What gives Glasgow its very specific visual-formal character is the use of sandstone as the prime construction material and the application of some late Georgian and largely Victorian design principles, adding to the perseverance of form and colour (the use of ochre sandstone first and red sandstone after 1880/90 generates consistent colour zones), pattern and texture.

4–04. *City block pattern of the city centre of Glasgow (excerpt from OS map 1861)*

4–05. *City block pattern of the Park and Woodlands area (excerpt from base map)*

4–06. Typical Glaswegian building types:

4–06. (a) terrace and tenement, Great George Street, Hillhead

4–06. (b) urban villas, Kirklee Road, Kelvinside

4–06. (d) office buildings, St Vincent Place, city centre

4–06. (c) multi-storey warehouse, Gardner's in Jamaica Street, city centre

4–06. (e) industrial building, Broomielaw, city centre

4.2 Glasgow's Development between the Wars

The first signs of a departure from the traditional Glaswegian development principles – incremental growth without much formal planning and urban design, the grid, the perimeter block and high-density development – can be seen immediately after the First World War in a period during which the Corporation provided new housing in form of cottages and flats. To accommodate the new housing estates the city area is expanded from 7,763 ha (1912) to 11,942 ha (1925) *(Fig. 4.08)*; by 1926 the total population of the city reaches 1,090,380, but the gross population density reduces from around 110 pph in 1912 to 91.31 pph (Glasgow City Council, 1997/98, *Factsheet 2*).

Introduction of the Garden Suburb

In one programme of inter-war development house types and settlement layouts were based on the principles of the garden suburb. Density of these settlements is relatively low in comparison to earlier tenement or terraced development and the city starts to sprawl. This development has been well covered by other publications (see Reed, 1993, chapter 8; Horsley, 1990, chapter 2) and only its most important design principles need to be mentioned here.

4–07. Living above the shop, Great Western Road, Woodlands

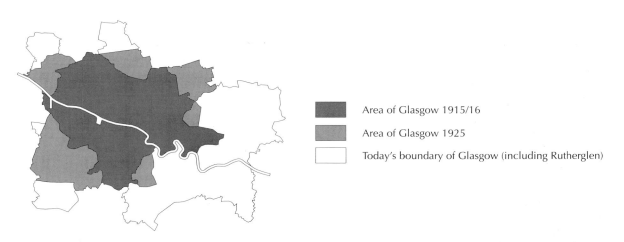

◼ Area of Glasgow 1915/16

▨ Area of Glasgow 1925

☐ Today's boundary of Glasgow (including Rutherglen)

4–08. Glasgow: city expansion by 1925 (based on Glasgow City Council, 1997/98, Factsheet 1)

4–09. *Plan configuration of Knightswood (excerpt from base map)*

The plan configuration of these inter-war garden suburbs is immediately recognisable, with their 'organic' shapes of loosely developed urban blocks and fragmented enclosure of streets *(Fig. 4.09)*. Despite the low density and the chance of good landscaping, the use of only a few different types of houses in the 'ordinary' schemes results in a limited visual and spatial variety if not a degree of dullness *(Fig. 4.10)*. There are some modernistic designs for private housing, but they are difficult to find and, being suburban villas, had little influence on urban form (McKean, 1993, p. 138). Owing to the low population density the new areas do not afford quality retail outlets. Community facilities in the new garden suburbs are somewhat scarce and consist usually of a number of small shops *(Fig. 4.11)*. However, the new estates provided family accommodation, and the quality of housing is enhanced through suitably sized front and rear garden spaces. It is not surprising, therefore, that many of these areas are still successful today.

New Tenement Development

In parallel to the development of garden suburbs, the Corporation used tenement housing and perimeter block configuration, largely for economic reasons, with

4–10. *Street in Knightswood South with semi-detached and terraced family cottages*

4–11. *Neighbourhood shops in Knightswood South*

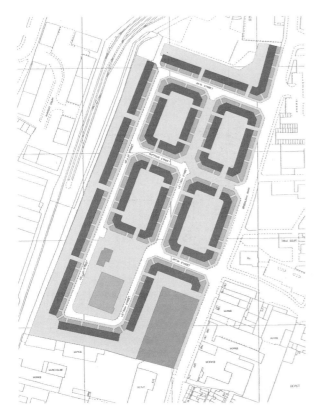

4–12. *Tenement development of the inter-war period in Govan (excerpt from base map)*

buildings generally only three storeys high and immediately recognisable in plan form through the diagonally cut corners of the blocks *(Fig. 4.12)*. Again, layouts and designs are fairly standardised, with window, door and other elements shared, and many of these tenements are built with Wilson blocks of rather indifferent colour and other poor properties. The tenement schemes generally provide well-designed flats and achieve a higher density of population than the cottages, but landscaping is poor and the consequences of all these features are monotonous, visually impoverished and often rather depressing tenement areas *(Fig. 4.13)*.

Effect of Inter-war Development on the City

All these new garden suburb or tenement housing areas are conceived as villages, often spatially isolated from other development clusters, thus exacerbating the fragmented character of the city's urban fabric. But these new villages no longer have, or even can afford, a horizontal and vertical mixture of uses; there are no high streets with shops, only occasionally some simple single-storey structures that accommodate a few small shops with little variety of goods. Distances to facilities beyond those catering for day-to-day needs grow and hence comes the need to travel to further away places. Another feature is that these areas accommodate primarily people of the same social and income levels, either middle-class in the semi-detached cottages and

4–13. Tenement blocks of the inter-war period in Kelvindale Road, Maryhill

terraces of the garden suburbs, or working-class in the new tenements. Poor management and maintenance of many if not all of the tenement areas, together with the concentration of low-income groups, result in what will soon be the city's new slum areas.

Comparison with Inter-war Housing in Berlin

If compared with the corresponding inter-war housing programme in, for instance, Berlin, Glasgow's approach to housing provision in this period, well motivated as it was, appears to lack imagination and design quality. In Berlin the settlements built between 1924 and 1932, and restored as part of the International Building Exhibition (IBA Berlin, 1984) – among others the Horseshoe Settlement Britz, the Forest Settlement Zehlendorf, Onkel Tom's Hütte, Siemensstadt, the White City – involve Germany's most formidable young architects at the time, especially Bruno Taut, Hugo Häring, Hans Scharoun, Otto Salvisberger, Walter Gropius, to name but the most significant. The explanation by Director

4–14. Tenement block of the inter-war period in the Forest Settlement, Zehlendorf, Berlin

Linneke of Gehag (one of the house-building companies) of the choice of these architects is revealing: 'We work with these consistent modern architects because we are a movement of tomorrow, a forward movement, and we cannot, therefore, build with architects of yesterday' (Linneke, 1926, author's translation).

The Berlin settlements are placed strategically to have access to the underground railway. The settlements have a community centre with shops and other facilities. The earlier schemes at Britz and Zehlendorf provide a mixture of two-storey family houses and flats in tenements, and the architecture as well as the landscaping is of very high quality; they also retain the traditional principles of urban blocks and perimeter development with medium high density *(Fig. 4.14).* These two schemes also introduce a colour scheme that contributes much to the friendliness and visual variety of the settlements. Only the later schemes, e.g. Siemensstadt and Weiße Stadt, introduce row houses, use more white surfaces and have no terraced family houses. (In Glasgow some influences of the Modernist movement on the design of housing become apparent only after the Second World War.)

Financing of the schemes is provided in a partnership approach by national and local government (through tax and direct subsidies), co-operatives, the trade union organisation, the workers' bank, social security, building societies. Because of the quality of urban design, architecture and landscaping these settlements have remained popular to the present day. The same can be said only about Glasgow's garden suburb area, with most if not all of the family houses now in private ownership, whereas many of the inter-war tenement areas are today's slums.

4.3 Glasgow in the 1950s, 1960s and Early 1970s

Immediately after the Second World War major rethinking of the city started all over Europe, and Glasgow was no exception. Even by 1938 the city area had expanded considerably from 11,942 ha in 1926 to 17,735 ha *(Fig. 4.15),* and programmes were developed after the war to decant people from overcrowded areas into new towns, to redevelop slum areas and to build a considerable amount of housing in new estates. The end result of these policies was that the total city population shrank from 1,090,380 in 1926 to 622,333 in 1995 (within the 1995 political boundary excluding Rutherglen; compare Glasgow City Council, 1997/98, Factsheet 2), and the gross population density was dramatically reduced from 91.31 pph in 1926 to 35.09 pph in 1995.

There are several reasons why a new approach to urban regeneration was considered essential: the need to provide new housing for those living in the tenement/industrial districts, which were declared to be slum areas to be demolished, and to replace war damage; the advent of mass car ownership, which necessitated an appropriate road network; and generally the view shared with the Modernist movement that the traditional city does not provide a suitable environment for people and needs to be replaced by a new urban morphology, the park with free-standing buildings in it (see Reed, 1993, chapter 9; Horsley, 1990, chapter 3).

A new and rather grand planning and urban design approach was applied: a wholesale review of the city, its transport network, its population density, its morphology and urban form, and almost all of this review was done in-house. A few 'famous' architects were involved, e.g. Basil Spence in the Gorbals with a scheme quite obviously inspired by Le Corbusier *(Fig. 4.16).* It was demolished in 1996.

It should not be forgotten that the approach to regenerating the city was clearly motivated by strong social and moral ideas: to relieve the pressure for housing by building new municipal houses, and to prepare the city for mass car ownership (see Watson, 1987). The Clyde Valley Plan of 1946, prepared for a committee of all

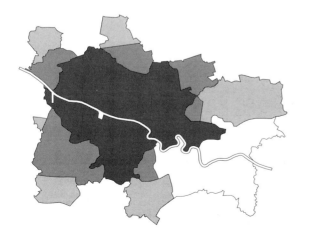

Area of Glasgow 1915/16

Area of Glasgow 1925

Area of Glasgow 1938

Today's boundary of Glasgow (including Rutherglen)

4–15. Glasgow: city area expansion by 1938 (based on Glasgow City Council, 1997/98, Factsheet 1)

4–16. *Queen Elizabeth Square, Glasgow, by architect Basil Spence*

local authorities in the area in response to the over-crowded conditions in slum areas, recommended 'planned decentralisation of population and industry' (Watson, 1987, p. 4).

Reducing housing densities and shortage and providing better housing conditions was a major priority of the city regeneration policy. Three plans contributed to this: decentralisation of population, which would be achieved with the help of new towns with 'overspill' agreement, in order to reduce housing demand to a degree; new housing development in peripheral estates; and the comprehensive development of much of the old tenement/industrial areas. Comprehensive development would provide an opportunity to prepare the city for mass car ownership and develop the necessary road infrastructure.

Comprehensive Development Areas and Peripheral Estates

For new and better housing the Development Plan of 1951 defined 31 inner-city areas with a concentration of slum housing for comprehensive development (Watson, 1987, p. 5). Also planned were four peripheral estates at the very edge of the city *(Fig. 4.17)*. These areas would make provision for new street patterns, shops, open space, schools and other community facilities. Land uses were separated to improve the quality of housing areas.

However rigorous the plans for new towns, comprehensive development areas (CDAs) with reduced population densities, and peripheral estates, the results were not only the decanting of people and the destruction of existing communities, the city lost many skilled people

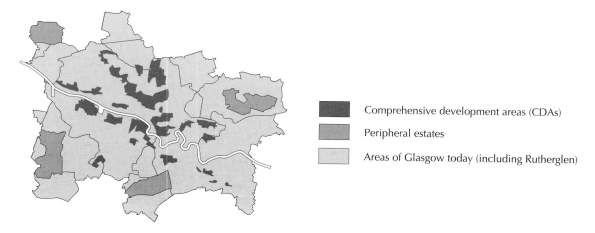

■ Comprehensive development areas (CDAs)

▨ Peripheral estates

▫ Areas of Glasgow today (including Rutherglen)

4–17. *Glasgow's comprehensive development areas (CDAs) and peripheral estates (based on Watson, 1987, maps 5A and 5B)*

and many viable businesses (Watson, 1987, p. 5). Many of the remaining industries were in decline and unemployment rose steadily. The city corporation had no specific interest in private housing, and its programmes for CDAs and peripheral estates resulted in a high concentration of lower-income households in specific areas of the city north, east and south of the linear central area and at the very city edges. New housing schemes at the periphery, though first raising the basic standards of living, failed to provide sufficient numbers of workplaces, services and facilities to render the estates self-supporting entities or 'towns', and they soon degenerated into deprived areas.

In spatial and formal terms, the Modern movement-inspired plans for CDAs largely rejected the traditional perimeter block development and the traditional height of terraces and tenements, which was up to four storeys. The streets were no longer enclosed, and the areas between free-standing buildings were neither private nor public but 'lost spaces' (see Trancik, 1986, figs 2.1 and 2.2). This resulted in the loss of interaction between people in streets and people in buildings, and streets and open spaces became deserted and to some extent dangerous *(Fig. 4.18)*.

In the CDAs and, to an extent, in the peripheral estates the traditional height restriction of housing to four storeys was thrown overboard, largely on the basis of the false argument that high-rise was essential in order to achieve the required densities and economic scale of production (Hall, 1990, p. 223). Most new

4–18. Lost space between high-rise blocks, Sighthill

4–19. High-rise blocks in Sighthill

high-rise schemes provided a density similar to if not lower than that of those they actually replaced. High-rise was even used in areas where it was clearly stated policy to reduce density. According to Markus, densities in Glasgow's CDAs 'were to be reduced from 450 persons per acre (in odd spots as high as 750) to 164, with a few local higher densities, such as the 200 resulting from the thirty-one-storey Red Road blocks in Sighthill' (Markus, 1993, p. 157). So a scheme with the tallest high-rise blocks in Europe achieved less than 50% of the population density of the same area before comprehensive development. There are many similar schemes with a high concentration of people in high-rise blocks, but they generally incorporate, and are surrounded by, large amounts of open land and as a result the population density is reduced considerably. Springburn to the north of the city centre accommodates a large cluster of high-rise housing (Fig. 4.19) but the overall gross population density of the area is 37.4 persons per hectare, i.e. only slightly above the average population density in Glasgow (calculated over the entire city area).

Housing provision in the peripheral estates is somewhat different. The plans for these estates are based on the principle of the garden suburb when it comes to overall density and the provision of green space. The built form, however, is largely tenemental, generally four-storey housing blocks, occasionally interspersed with high-rise flats. With the application of four-storey tenements the density should theoretically be relatively high, but in reality density is rather low as a result of the vast internal courtyards of tenement blocks and the enormous green areas in between which, owing to the lack of any proper landscaping, represent neither parks nor sports grounds nor gardens and are largely unused (Fig. 4.20). The gross population density of a traditional nineteenth-century tenement area can be as high as 128.7 persons per hectare (pph), as, for instance, in Govanhill (Glasgow City Council, 1995); that of Drum-chapel, one of the four peripheral estates at the north-western edge of the city, is only 45.4 pph (calculation based on Glasgow City Council, 1995).

One of the major problems in the peripheral estates is the very high concentration of low-income households, and soon after the tenants had become accustomed to new bathrooms and kitchens and good ventilation and exposure to sun, they became aware of the many shortcomings. The peripheral estates are equipped with centres accommodating retail and other services and facilities. But these centres, cheaply built and badly landscaped, provide poor service and choice to people with little disposable income, and many of the shops are now defunct (Fig. 4.21). The new tenements may initially have provided reasonable flats in comparison to those in the old slum areas, but poor design and construction, lack of landscaping, bad management and poor maintenance caused the peripheral estates to deteriorate into ghettos for the underprivileged. Those who can afford it move into more privileged districts, causing the population density in the peripheral estates to decline and retail and services to become even less viable.

Road-building Programme

Another major regeneration programme targeted the city's transport problems, with roads inadequate to cope with the expected increase in private vehicular transport. One answer to the problem was to withdraw the old tramcars from service (1962) to free the road for the car. Another answer was to build new expressways and

4–20. Aerial photo of Castlemilk (aerial photograph reproduced with kind permission of Glasgow Development Agency.© Scottish Enterprise)

4–21. Shopping centre, Easterhouse

motorways. Yet at the same time there was no convincing plan for the improvement of public transport; in fact the decommissioning of the tramcars removed a very good public transport system. The lack of a public transport policy is all the more astonishing in view of the high percentage of households that would not in the near future, or ever, be able to afford a car. Even today 66.7% of households have no car (Glasgow City Council, 1995).

Two years before Copenhagen's planners returned from the USA, decided not to go along with city development driven by vehicular transport and introduced their 'Finger Plan', which restricts city expansion to five public transport routes (Hartoft-Nielson, 1993, pp. 1–25), the Bruce Plan (Bruce, 1945) suggested that

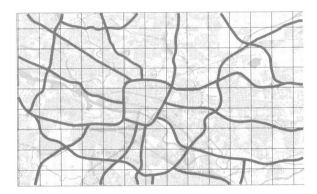

4–22. Motorway and expressway plan of 1965 (redrawn after the Glasgow District Council's final proposal of 1965)

4–23. The M8 motorway at Charing Cross

Glasgow must be comprehensively modified to prepare for mass car ownership. The plan proposed an inner motorway box – more than a ring – around a newly defined city centre and a number of roads forming a kind of grid and outer ring mainly to the south of the centre. This plan was accompanied by the 'modest' suggestion of demolishing the entire historical city centre and replacing it with free-standing blocks in the mode of Hilberseimer's ideal city. Fortunately only small parts of this plan were implemented and the city centre remains largely intact. The original road plan was revised and modified in a number of stages (see Markus, 1993, p. 160). The final proposal of 1965 suggested an inner motorway ring which is fed by radial routes from all directions; there is also an outer ring *(Fig. 4.22)*. In a first phase the northern and western sections of the inner ring formed by the M8 were built, bulldozing through the urban fabric between centre and the Park/Woodlands area *(Fig. 4.23)*. Today the road system, no longer exactly following the 1965 plan, is still being expanded, with a proposal for a southern tangent (the M74), and part of the 1965 plan, a motorway to the south-west through Pollok Park (the M77), has been implemented. The current condition is illustrated in Chapter 5.

Conclusions

Despite the large-scale and rigorously planned and 'designed' approach the overall outcome of comprehensive development and new housing estates at the city's periphery is in many ways an unmitigated disaster. In social terms, many of the CDAs and peripheral estates are deprived areas. In urban design terms, the city has maintained some of its high-quality historical areas, specifically in the central linear area and some of the early inner suburbs, but these areas are now surrounded by repetitive and sprawling garden suburbs, ugly high-rise and poor-quality tenement development with poorly designed and randomly scattered tower blocks dominating much of the city's skyline *(Fig. 4.24)*. The city has lost much of its identity and about half its population but has hugely expanded in area as a result of the city boundary expansions of 1925 (inter-war housing schemes) and 1938 (mainly accommodating the peripheral estates). During the inter-war and immediate post-war periods of urban transformation the city took on what today many call unsustainable characteristics.

4.4 Consolidation of the Old City but new Development at Random: the 1970s and 1980s

The 1970s brought a change in attitude towards the historical areas of the city, perhaps as a reaction to the failure of the CDAs and peripheral estates: the quality of the city centre and the old tenement and terraced areas with their rigorous block structure was rediscovered and newly appreciated. The conservation movement started tentatively in 1964 with the foundation of the New Glasgow Society, which was interested in the city's environment and attempted to publicise Glasgow's historical architecture. The society's idea of 'renewal through conservation' did not, however, find support then. But soon the conservation movement became consolidated through a number of actions (see Martin, 1993, pp. 167–84):

4–24. Today's city skyline, Glasgow (view from Kelvindale looking north-west)

- The Scottish Civic Trust was set up in 1967.

- The Civic Amenity Act was passed by Parliament in 1967 giving statutory force to the designation of conservation areas.

- The Glasgow Corporation's Amenity Liaison Committee was set up in 1972 to establish a dialogue between the Corporation and amenity societies.

- The report *Conservation in Glasgow* by Lord Esher, published in 1971, recommended among other policies nine additional conservation areas.

- The Town and Country Planning (Scotland) Act of 1972 gave legal protection to almost 800 buildings of special architectural or historic interest in Glasgow.

- The Planning Policy Report *Conservation* published by the Glasgow Corporation in 1974 introduced historic building grant aid and other conservation policies and proposals.

In parallel a programme of tenement rehabilitation was instigated. A storm in 1968 had caused serious damage to about 16,000 tenement properties, and the quickest way of providing habitable accommodation was to repair the existing building stock. In 1969 ASSIST, a research group at the University of Strathclyde's Department of Architecture and Building Science, developed a tenement improvement programme for the installation of basic services, bathrooms and kitchens. In 1972 the first community-based housing association was established at central Govan. The Housing (Scotland) Act of 1974 enabled housing associations registered with the Housing Corporation to obtain financial support for wholesale tenement rehabilitation programmes and introduced the concept of 'action areas'. Between 1974 and 1990, Glaswegian housing associations renovated over 18,000 tenement flats (see Martin, 1993, pp. 184–6).

All this added up to an extensive programme of consolidation, repair and revitalisation of much of the remaining historical fabric in the central linear areas and some of the inner suburbs, and this in turn saved Glasgow's image as an exceptional Victorian city. Next to the programme of the restoration of nineteenth-century tenements, the rehabilitation of the Merchant City and many other related projects are especially impressive as the quality and liveliness of the historical areas have much improved *(Fig. 4.25a, b)*.

(a)

(b)

4–25. Consolidation of the historical areas of Glasgow that survived comprehensive development: (a) facade retention in the Merchant City; (b) tenement rehabilitation in Dennistoun

4–26. Glasgow's new sheriff's court south of the river

(a)

(b)

4–27. Out-of-town retail park development: (a) The Forge (aerial photo reproduced with kind permission of Glasgow Development Agency. © Scottish Enterprise); (b) Clydebank Shopping Centre

The consolidation of the historical fabric did not, however, coincide with a return to traditional planning and design principles for new development. There was no return to the grid structure and the perimeter block development principle, which both achieve the integration of disparate and incremental projects. Many new schemes, including important public buildings and flagship projects of the city, remain isolated events. There was no strategic plan, no design framework for the integration of individual projects, and many of them float in no man's land and do not contribute to the activation of public streets and squares *(Fig. 4.26)*.

Later, during the 1980s and as a consequence of the

Thatcherite enterprise culture philosophy, strategic planning disappeared altogether from the vocabulary of urban development to make way for a *laissez-faire* attitude in which the city is shaped by market forces. The main argument was that control of market forces would not permit them to function effectively and would, therefore, stifle urban development (Hall, 1988, pp. 359ff). So they were frequently left to do whatever they wanted to do. In parallel, much retail moved out of urban districts into out-of-town or in-between-town parks *(Fig. 4.27a, b)* or, fighting to survive in the city centre, disappeared into introverted shopping malls *(Fig. 4.28a, b)* with dead service zones fronting public streets

(a)

(b)

4–28. Inner-city retail development: *(a) St Enoch Centre at Howard Street; (b) the Buchanan Galleries model*

4–29. Enterprise zone at Port Glasgow

and squares. Many commercial and industrial enterprises moved into business and industrial parks, often in enterprise zones *(Fig. 4.29)* outside the city boundary, and people moved out as well. Even some university departments and related industries moved into science parks. The disentanglement of uses, separating out into individual isolated places even more radically than at previous stages of urban development, left many urban areas even less activated and generated even more need for transport. And as population densities shrank, the most suitable form of transport was frequently the car.

Housing too contributed to the dispersal of the city. The public sector had ceased to build new housing, the private sector generated semi-detached or terraced family housing around culs-de-sac, 'lollipop' housing of very low density and often at the very edge of the city, which as a result continued to sprawl *(Fig. 4.30a, b).*

4.5 The City Today

The legacy of inter-war housing schemes, of comprehensive development and peripheral estates and of largely uncontrolled development during much of the 1980s and 1990s is a city that shows all the symptoms of unsustainability summarised in section 1.2. These symptoms are briefly illustrated.

Uneven Population Density and Sprawl

With the exception of the historical high-density areas, the urban fabric is thinly spread over a vast area *(Fig. 4.31).* The overall gross population density of Glasgow (city boundary) is not particularly low (about 58.5 persons per hectare over the 60% of the city area that is

developed; Glasgow City Council, 1995) but is rather unevenly distributed. The historical areas of the West End and some districts in the south reach gross population densities of up to 129 pph but suburban areas may reach densities as low as 10 pph (Glasgow City Council, 1995) *(Fig. 4.32).* This indicates that in some areas there is considerable spare capacity or, seen the other way round, that there is a considerable amount of land that could be transformed into green open space to become part of the city's hinterland if the population density in the developed areas were to be increased to the average of 60 pph which is considered to be the required threshold value. I shall return to the question of density when investigating a more sustainable structure for the conurbation of Glasgow in Chapter 5.

Functional Zoning

Many of the city's services and facilities, and with them workplaces, are concentrated in the relatively small city centre, which is surrounded by housing areas which are to a very large extent mono-use areas, dormitory places; the exceptions again are the historical districts. Despite the surplus capacity of the city much of the new private-sector housing is built on greenfield sites, frequently at the edge of the city or conurbation *(Fig. 4.33)* rather than on brownfield sites and gap sites in inner suburban areas, and this contributes to further sprawl of the city and car dependency of the citizens.

Despite the government U-turn regarding the location of retail (PPG6) and public transport (PPG13), out-of-town retailing is still mushrooming, providing for those who are mobile, specifically those with a car, and ignoring those who are less mobile and the more than 60% of the population without a car. As a result, many

(a)

(b)

4–30. *'Lollipop' housing, frequently at the edge of the city. (a) case study estate layout from* A Design Guide for Residential Areas, *Essex County Council, 1973 (reproduced by kind permission of Essex County Council); (b) a recent housing scheme off Kelvindale Road, Glasgow*

high street retail outlets are closing *(Fig. 4.34)* and more local provision, including schools, is lost, which in turn exacerbates the need to travel to further away facilities. In the city centre the concentration of city-wide activities and workplaces leads to serious congestion and pollution; some of the central streets are said to be the most polluted in Europe *(Fig. 4.35).*

Highway planning is still ongoing despite the worldwide experience that providing more roads does not, in the medium to long term, solve the problem of congestion but generates more traffic. Furthermore, as in the past, highway planning is carried out without an integrated view of districts and their role, and there does not seem to be co-ordination with public transport

4–31. *The sprawling city: aerial photograph of Garntyre looking east (aerial photograph, reproduced with kind permission of the Glasgow Development Agency.© Scottish Enterprise)*

4–32. Uneven distribution of population in Glasgow, today's boundaries including Rutherglen (based on Glasgow City Council, 1995)

4–33. Continuing development of greenfield sites

4–34. High street shops boarded up: eastern end of Great Western Road

4–35. Congested and polluted city
centre roads: Renfield Street

Glasgow's most deprived areas

Area of Glasgow today (including Rutherglen)

4–36. The most deprived areas of
Glasgow (based on Glasgow City
Council, 1995)

4–37. Rehabilitation of the
peripheral Easterhouse estate

planning, park-and-ride and other efforts to keep cars out of the dense city centre areas and to minimise car dependency in other urban areas.

Social Stratification

The social stratification of the city continues. The city is an agglomeration of ghettos for the rich and ghettos for the poor, with the rich and mobile in advantaged areas which they can afford and the poor and badly mobile in disadvantaged areas because they cannot afford to live anywhere else. Many of the tenement housing areas developed around the 1930s and many of the CDAs are today part of seriously deprived areas *(Fig. 4.36)*. There are ongoing programmes of rehabilitation of peripheral estates and other problem areas *(Fig. 4.37)*, but improvement is carried out without much of a study of the costs and benefits in the long term and without tackling the structural and socio-economic problems of these areas effectively (Reed, 1993, pp. 219ff). It can therefore be expected that much of the improvement carried out over the past two or so decades will have no long-term effect and that in the end the old problems will prevail. In some areas deprivation and dilapidation are so intense that demolition is seen as the only answer, without taking into account that with demolition the problem is only shifted elsewhere rather than solved.

Spatial and Formal Incoherence

In terms of form and image Glasgow is well structured and well designed, with legible paths, districts and mon-

uments, only in historical areas. Other areas suffer from a mixture of poor spatial structure, poor architecture and poor landscaping, and accordingly are imageless and without identity, and indistinguishable from other city areas *(Fig. 4.38)*.

Conclusions

Many believe that a city with such characteristics is not sustainable. Calls for visions and strategies are becoming louder, planning and design groups are being mobilised and debates are being organised to look at the city comprehensively and investigate strategies that might improve form and structure as well as the socio-economic conditions (e.g. University of Strathclyde River Clyde Conference 1996; GIA River Clyde workshop 1996; City of Glasgow Planning Department, design framework for Partick Riverside, etc.).

Needless to say, Glasgow is not the only city with such problems; in fact many cities in the UK have much worse problems and also lack Glasgow's remarkable qualities developed during the Victorian era. Glasgow has been selected to represent the post-industrial city for the very simple reason that it is 'at hand'.

Chapter 5 will discuss which city model can be applied to improve the considerable structural, functional, formal and image problems of such a city. The purpose of this discussion is to exemplify the viability of one of the macro-structures investigated in Chapter 3 and the applicability of the generally valid micro-structure of the city or conurbation to improve the existing, or generate a new, hierarchy of provision centres linked by a transport network.

4–38. Formal and spatial chaos north of Glasgow city centre: Garngad, Springburn, Sighthill (aerial photograph, reproduced with kind permission of the Glasgow Development Agency. © Scottish Enterprise)

References

Bruce, R. (1945) *First Planning Report to the Highways and Planning Committee of the Corporation of Glasgow*, 2 volumes, Glasgow Corporation, Glasgow.

Glasgow City Council (1995) *Ward Profiles*, Department of Planning and Development, Glasgow.

Glasgow City Council (1997/98) *Factsheets 1 and 2*, Department of Planning and Development, Glasgow.

Hall, P. (1988) *Cities of Tomorrow*, Blackwell, Oxford.

Hartoft-Nielson, P. (1993) The Danish experience: Copenhagen, in *The European City and Its Region: How Can the Co-ordination of Physical Planning Be Achieved?* International conference, Dublin, October 1993, organised by the Department of the Environment, Ireland, in conjunction with the Directorate-General for Regional Policies of the European Commission.

Horsley, M. (1990) *Tenements & Towers: Glasgow Working-Class Housing 1890–1990*, The Royal Commission on the Ancient and Historical Monuments of Scotland.

Internationale Bauausstellung Berlin (1984) *Siedlungen der zwanziger Jahre – heute, Vier Berliner Großsiedlungen 1924–1984*, Publica Verlagsgesellschaft, Berlin.

Linneke, R. (1926) Zwei Jahre GEHAG-Arbeit. *Wohnungswirtschaft, 3*.

McKean, C. (1993) Between the wars, in Reed, P. (ed.) *Glasgow: The Forming of the City*, Edinburgh University Press, Edinburgh.

Markus, T. (1993) Comprehensive development and housing, 1945–75, in Reed, P. (ed.) *Glasgow: The Forming of the City*, Edinburgh University Press, Edinburgh.

Martin, D.T. (1993) Conservation and restoration, in Reed, P. (ed.) *Glasgow: The Forming of the City*, Edinburgh University Press, Edinburgh.

Reed, P. (ed.) (1993) *Glasgow: The Forming of the City*, Edinburgh University Press, Edinburgh.

Trancik, R. (1986) *Finding Lost Space*, Van Nostrand Reinhold, New York.

Watson, J. (1987) Let Glasgow flourish: Glasgow's bold approach to urban renewal, paper presented at the 2nd Conference of the International Centre for Studies in Urban Design, Florence.

Application of Micro- and Macro-structure: The Case of Glasgow

5

Both the micro- and the macro-structures of the city models which were compared in Chapter 3 are abstract forms, and no city will ever resemble any of them. It is therefore essential to investigate the relevance of these structures for a real city and city region. This chapter examines the existing macro-structure for the city region of Glasgow and attempts to implement the hierarchical composition of the city's micro-structure in the Glasgow conurbation. One objective of this analytical and generative exercise is to establish whether any of the macro-structural city models investigated have any relevance to a real conurbation with its very specific development pattern and structure. Another objective is to establish to what degree the micro-structure of a sustainable city and city region can be implemented without major structural changes to the conurbation.

5.1 City Region

Glasgow is the largest city in a development belt stretching from the Firth of Clyde at its western end to the Firth

5–01. Figure-ground of the city region of Glasgow (based on OS Pathfinder maps)

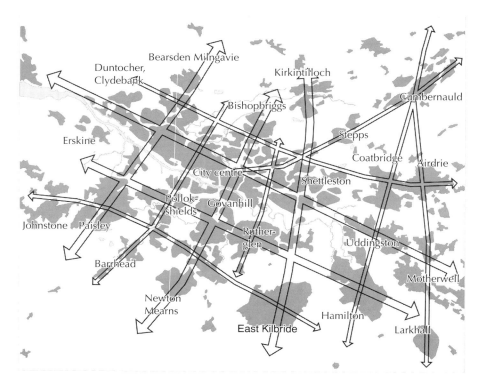

5–02. Development structure of the city region of Glasgow

of Forth in the east. The western part of this belt, the city region of Glasgow, is of particular interest here.

Figure-Ground of the City Region

The city region shows a rather typical post-industrial development structure: there are areas of concentrated development, but as a whole the region is an agglomeration of different development clusters of smaller and larger size which are more or less attached to each other *(Fig. 5.01)*. When one studies the plan configuration of this region, it is entirely unclear where Glasgow starts and where it ends. The concentration of development in the central area, and specifically north of the river, suggests where Glasgow might be located but one could not be sure about this without more detailed investigation. This indicates even at this early stage of investigation that planning and designing a development framework for the city of Glasgow on its own, as defined by its political boundaries, will not be sufficient in the search for a more sustainable city form and structure; the entire region needs to be considered. One may also conclude even at this stage that the model of a compact city in the form of Lynch's 'core city' may have little relevance for Glasgow and that the regional city model may suit best for a more sustainable form and structure for the entire region.

Development Structure of the City Region

When one analyses the city region more closely, a reasonably clear structure emerges *(Fig. 5.02)*.

The River Clyde divides the city region into a northern and southern area. North of the river, and following it roughly in east/west direction, there is a fairly continuous development belt; only its eastern end is somewhat fragmented. South of the river there is a second linear east/west development belt, but it is more fragmented than that to the north. These two belts constitute the central linear development area of the city region which is clearly influenced in its direction and development by the river.

The central east/west development belt is flanked to the north and south by highly fragmented development which is more attached to the central area to the north and more detached from it to the south. The development clusters of the city region also form major and minor development strips in north/south direction and one more diagonal development towards the north-east.

The principal pattern of the city region is accordingly a somewhat irregular grid of more continuous urban fabric in the linear east/west centre and more fragmented urban fabric towards the edges of the region.

Major Transport Routes in the City Region

The east/west and north/south development strips or belts of the city region follow major transport routes

5–03. *Major transport routes in the city region of Glasgow*

which also form a fairly irregular grid which deforms somewhat at the city region's eastern edge. There is also a diagonal route from the south-west to the north-east *(Fig. 5.03)*.

With this gridded primary transport structure all areas of the region are more or less equally accessible, and this may prove rather useful when reviewing the transport strategy for the conurbation of Glasgow.

At the intersections of the transport routes major development nodes, including the city centre of Glasgow, do already exist or could be formed, and this structure may again prove of considerable advantage when studying the micro-structure of the conurbation of Glasgow.

Structure of Linear Open Spaces

Another important feature of the city region of Glasgow is that a number of linear open spaces stretch right through the region and right into the central development zones *(Fig. 5.04)*. There is first of all the linear Clyde valley dividing the central linear development area of the region. There are less continuous linear green spaces in east/west direction between the central linear area and the outer northern and southern development clusters. Then there are several green wedges in north/south direction bringing open country right to the edges of the central linear development area.

The city region's development zones – which form a

somewhat irregular and (to the north, east and south) fragmented grid – are accordingly well intersected by linear open spaces, themselves forming a somewhat incomplete and fairly irregular semi-grid, separated from centre-east to north-west by the inner linear development area. The relationship of urban fabric and open country is accordingly very good: access from urban areas to open green space is easy and distance is reasonably short. Furthermore, as all major green spaces and wedges are directly linked to the country, a symbiotic relationship of the city region with nature can easily be established.

Conclusions

With such characteristics, the conurbation of Glasgow exemplifies a typical regional agglomeration of smaller and larger development units, partially continuous, partially fragmented. It does not seem conceivable that such a configuration could ever be restructured into a series of isolated 'compact cities' in the sense of autonomous 'core cities' without suburbs. Even the structures of the star and satellite city models have little in common with that of Glasgow's city region. With a primary transport grid and a secondary transport network (still to be investigated) as well as, potentially, primary and secondary centres at the intersections of transport routes and development strips, the city region of Glasgow possesses all major structural characteristics

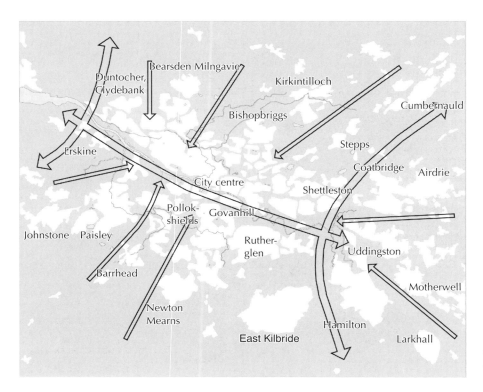

5–04. Structure of linear open spaces in the city region of Glasgow

of Lynch's polycentric net as illustrated by *Fig. 3.30*. As the potential functional, environmental and ecological advantages of this model have already been established in principle, there does not seem to be any reason why the existing network of routes and development clusters or zones should be changed – if such a change would be economically and socially viable at all. It also seems that the existing network of linkages may be of considerable advantage for the establishment of an efficient public and private transport structure which provides reasonably equal access to all conurbation areas. The grid is also the kind of structure that would allow a city region to grow and shrink, in adaptation to changing socio-economic conditions, without major upheaval. However, understanding of how the existing regional structure of urban fabric and open land can be reinforced and improved requires a more detailed investigation of the pattern, which may well lead to a suggestion of more compact development zones and clusters within the regional structure.

Having established the existing macro-structure of the city region of Glasgow, a polycentric net, we must now ascertain the detailed configuration of this structure and study the existing and the potential micro-structure of the conurbation.

5.2 The Existing Development Pattern of Greater Glasgow

Further investigation focuses on the central area of the city region, eliminating part of the more detached development clusters at the edges of the city region *(Fig. 5.05)*. The development clusters at the eastern edge of the city are well separated from the central-eastern ones; they have therefore all been cut off the area of investigation. The area beyond the western north/south development strip between Paisley and Milngavie has also been cut off because it is sparsely developed and the only significant cluster, Johnstone, is well separated from Paisley. The most northern development clusters, Milngavie, Kirkintilloch and Cumbernauld, have been clipped but their southern areas are still part of the detailed map. The same has been done with the most southern clusters, Newton Mearns, East Kilbride and Hamilton; only their northern parts are still on the map.

This somewhat unfortunate reduction of the area for detailed investigation was necessary primarily in order to guarantee the legible representation of the entire Greater Glasgow area down to the details of individual urban blocks and streets. The inclusion of the entire metropolitan area to the same level of detailed information would have been possible only if illustrations had been segmented or if a larger-scale representation

5–05. Reduction of the area under detailed investigation (shaded area)

had been possible. Segmentation was excluded because it would have considerably reduced the legibility and understanding of the area under investigation; a larger scale of representation was not possible.

In the following section, the existing structure of Greater Glasgow is investigated. Then an attempt is made to generate – on the basis of the existing development pattern and transport networks and the location of present neighbourhood centres and other centres of provision – a pattern of neighbourhoods, districts and towns with their respective centres and the primary and secondary transport networks that would link them with each other. All structural features of the resulting pattern are firmly based on the existing features of Greater Glasgow, and for that reason it was necessary to generate a reasonably accurate detailed representation of the conurbation with all existing streets and urban blocks.

Some of the Ordnance Survey Pathfinder maps (403/404, 416/417 and 430/431) used for that purpose were produced as long ago as 1978 and only partially revised during the 1980s, and will therefore inevitably exclude the representation of more recent development. However, for an investigation of a city's form and structure at conurbation level such changes, mainly of smaller scale, are of relatively little importance and can be ignored.

Existing Figure-Ground of Greater Glasgow

The investigation of the figure-ground of the city region *(Fig. 5.01)* has already illustrated the considerable degree of fragmentation of urban fabric into partially linked and partially segregated development clusters of larger or smaller scale. But in this region-wide figure-ground the developed areas were mapped without any detailed information of their spatial organisation and structure. It can therefore be expected that the detailed mapping of the plan configuration of Greater Glasgow may generate a picture of even greater fragmentation because now all details of the internal structure of development clusters are revealed. A base map has therefore been constructed which represents – next to the rivers, which make recognition of the conurbation easier – the solid/void pattern of all built-up areas with their structure of urban blocks, streets and squares *(Fig. 5.06)*. Not represented in the base map are green spaces, in order to highlight the pattern generated by the urban fabric. Industrial areas are represented but toned down. The main reason for this is that the majority of industrial areas – either along the River Clyde or along other rivers and canals or railway lines – have no clear access system, and only a few of them (e.g. Hillington) have a kind of urban block structure. Many of these areas are also part of the linear open spaces (like the River Clyde) dividing the development clusters or belts

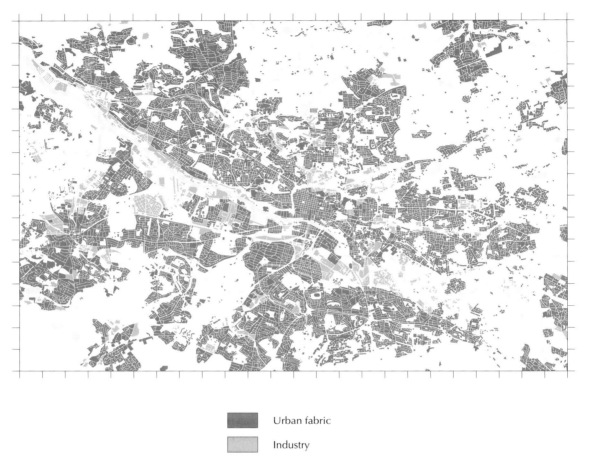

Urban fabric

Industry

5–06. *Figure-ground of the conurbation of Glasgow (based on OS Pathfinder maps)*

of the conurbation. Industrial areas generally do not, therefore, contribute to the morphology of built-up areas, but they frequently act as a buffer between development clusters.

The resulting figure-ground confirms that Greater Glasgow is an agglomeration of linked districts and towns, but it also illustrates that the development clusters themselves are fragmented to a greater or lesser degree. The linear south-east/north-west development belt north of the River Clyde (already delineated in *Fig. 5.02*) shows a degree of continuity of the urban fabric, specifically westwards from the city centre, but even this area incorporates several larger green river and canal spaces, which reinforces the impression of fragmentation. The task ahead is to find out what micro-structure exists in this fragmented conurbation and how it can be improved.

Existing Vehicular Transport Network

The figure-ground on its own shows several clear circulation routes, but it is difficult to distinguish between roads and railway lines. Therefore the figure-ground map is reversed into a street map and the major vehicular traffic routes – such as motorways and expressways as well as other major access roads – are highlighted *(Fig. 5.07)*. The map reveals a rather interesting situation.

There are two major east–west routes (motorways and expressways), one north, the other south of the River Clyde. They provide access to areas to their north and south but are also inter-city routes linking the conurbation with other eastern and western areas. Both are linked by the north–south stretch of the M8 immediately west of the city centre (this route extends further to the south-west via the M77) and by other north–south motorway connections at the very eastern and western edges of the conurbation (the latter just indicated in the

	Urban fabric
	Industry
———	Primary transport routes
– – – – –	Clyde Tunnel

5–07. Existing vehicular transport routes in the conurbation of Glasgow (based on OS Pathfinder maps)

top left of the map). Other secondary north–south links connect the northern and western south-east/north-west routes. There is also a diagonal route linking the city centre with the north-eastern area of the conurbation (Cumbernauld). Major and secondary routes form an irregular grid, as was expected when the pattern of the city region was investigated *(Fig. 5.03)*.

In the area between the east and the city centre the northern major south-east/north-west traffic route is located between development clusters and is therefore not expected to cause major conflicts with built-up areas on either side. But between the city centre and the north-west the route leads right through the most densely and most continuously developed northern south-east/north-west development belt of the conurbation (via Great Western Road), and this must lead to considerable conflicts, congestion and pollution, specifically because the stretch between the city centre

and the West End also accommodates retail and a variety of other services and facilities. It will be essential to study an alternative route for this stretch of the primary vehicular transport grid. The southern major south-east/north-west route (the M74 from the south-east to the city centre (not yet completed), the M8 from the city centre to the west) is continuously located between development strips and clusters and should not cause major concern for the urban areas on either side.

The transport net as a whole seems to provide a good structure for access to all areas of the conurbation despite the fact that the north–south links are somewhat sporadic and there is consequently a serious lack of river crossings in between the major routes, which are fairly large distances apart. It is also important to note that the majority of these routes exclude local public transport other than buses. The viability of a narrower grid of routes, including new river crossings, and of the

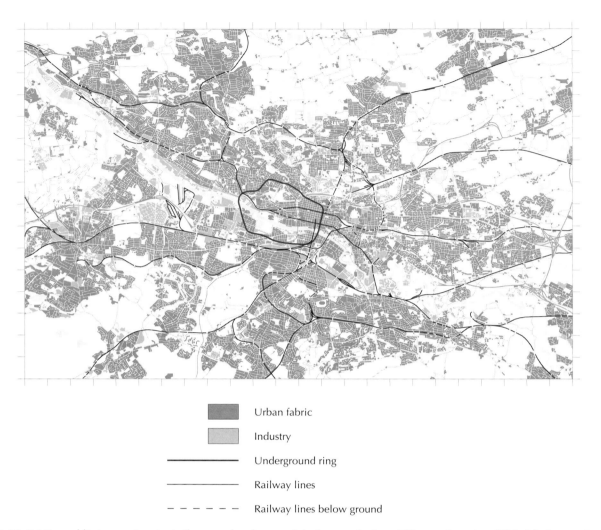

5–08. *Existing public transport routes (railways and underground) in the conurbation of Glasgow (based on OS Pathfinder maps)*

▨	Urban fabric
▨	Industry
——	Underground ring
——	Railway lines
– – – –	Railway lines below ground

combination of public and private transport on the routes needs to be investigated later.

Existing Public Transport Network

Now that we have gained an understanding of the kind of grid system which the private transport routes form, the public transport network needs to be investigated. Of specific interest at this stage is the network formed by existing railway lines and the underground railway, because these represent rigid systems in locational terms. Bus routes are presently excluded because they can take any configuration. The resulting map *(Fig. 5.08)* shows a very interesting pattern. There appear to be a number of east–west railway lines, two of

them north and two south of the River Clyde. The inner of the northern lines roughly follows the river from the north-west to the city centre and from there to the east is located between the northern and southern strips of the south-east/north-west development zone. The outer of the northern lines is located roughly between the northern south-east/north-west development strip and the northern suburbs. The inner of the southern east–west railway lines follows the major east–west vehicular route between the inner and outer south-east/north-west development zone; the outer line is somewhat fragmented, connecting southern suburbs. With the exception of the central area of the conurbation, the railway lines are generally located between development clusters, though targeting the centres of

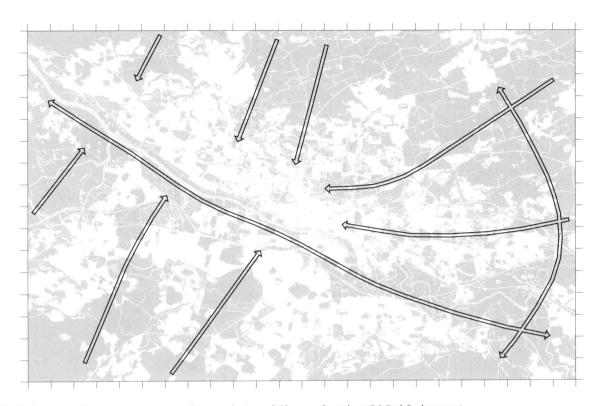

5–09. Structure of linear open spaces in the conurbation of Glasgow (based on OS Pathfinder maps)

some of the bigger town clusters. They can therefore be expected to play only a limited role for local connections inside and between urban districts.

Of particular interest are the north–south connections between these east–west railway lines, which are much less consistent and – with the exception of one in the West End – concentrated in the central area of the conurbation. This is understandable because the major task of these railway lines is to link with the stations in the city centre despite the kind of grid they apparently form. This, however, means that north–south public transport links (other than bus routes) are missing outside the central area of the conurbation, and this can be expected to cause difficulties of access at a local level between development clusters throughout the conurbation.

The underground ring links the city centre with the central section of the inner northern and southern south-east/north-west development strips and is therefore of little significance for the conurbation at large. From this study it becomes clear that what is obviously missing is a secondary system of public transport intermediate between railways and buses, for instance a light rail transit network. The potential for such a system and the location of its lines will be investigated in due course.

Structure of Linear Open Spaces

As we have seen *(Fig. 5.04)*, the city region has a number of linear wedges of open space located between development strips and clusters *(Fig. 5.09)*. There is first of all the River Clyde valley, which divides the inner south-east/north-west development zone into a northern and southern strip. This open space is continuous but narrows down to a shallow ribbon in the city centre, the only area in which the urban fabric forms a hard river edge north and potentially south of the river. The river space east and west of the city centre accommodates a major proportion of the conurbation's industry. A second linear open space in a south-east/north-west direction is located south of the river and separates the inner from the outer south-east/north-west development zone. This green open space accommodates the major existing and planned southern vehicular transport route (the M74 and M8) running parallel to railway lines in a south-east/north-west direction. A third linear open space in the same direction, located east of the city centre, splits the northern inner development strip right from the eastern edge of the conurbation to the city centre. It accommodates a railway line, some industry and other large-scale uses.

▨	Urban fabric
▨	Industry
▬▬▬▬	Motorway
------------	Primary transport routes
▬▬▬▬	Railway lines
▬▬▬▬	Underground ring

5–10. *Superimposition of figure-ground and the networks of public and private transport (based on OS Pathfinder maps)*

There are a number of open space wedges roughly in a north–south direction. They are located between the primary and secondary north–south development zones and link the open country right to the inner or outer south-east/north-west development zones but are only occasionally continuous all the way through the conurbation in the form of a river valley or a railway line.

In addition to the linear open spaces, there are a large number of smaller green pockets inside the development clusters and strips. The smaller of the open linear and pocket spaces need to be investigated at a district level. The conurbation accordingly has good links with the open countryside and a symbiotic relationship with nature could easily be established.

Seeing it All Together

When the figure-ground, the networks of public transport and the grid of primary and secondary vehicular traffic routes are superimposed, the pattern found in the city region is clearly reflected in that of the conurbation of Glasgow *(Fig. 5.10)*. The existing structure of the conurbation is not at all concentric-radial as was obviously the intention of transportation plans developed between 1947 and 1965 (see section 4.3 and *Fig. 4.22*) but consists of south-east/north-west and north/south strips or zones of development which necessitate major transport routes forming a somewhat irregular grid. Of particular importance will be the further investigation of a public transport network at a district level which provides better and more even access to development

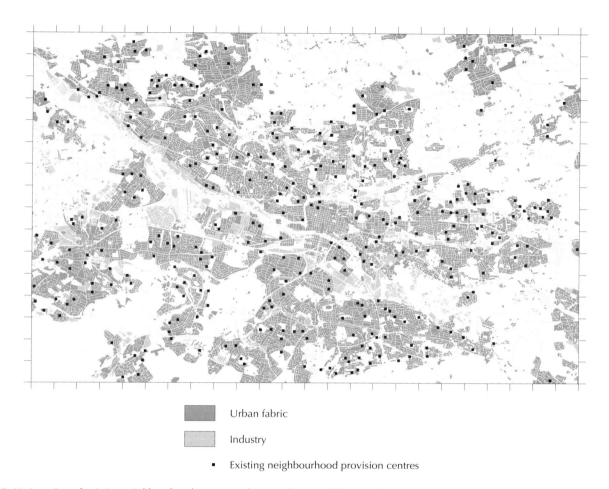

Urban fabric

Industry

▪ Existing neighbourhood provision centres

5–11. Location of existing neighbourhood centres in the conurbation of Glasgow (based on OS Pathfinder maps)

areas within the north/south and south-east/north-west development strips. Some nodes do already exist at their intersections, others need to be established. However, what needs to be explored prior to such a transport network is the existing and potentially improved or developed micro-structure of this pattern; this will lead to an expanded public transport network that supports the micro-structure; and this exploration is carried out in what follows.

5.3 Search for a Micro-structure of Provision Centres and Transport Linkages

In this part of the investigation of the conurbation of Glasgow the existing micro-structure of the city is analysed in order to find out whether the hierarchical structure of provision centres and linkages discussed earlier (see section 3.3 and *Figs. 3.08, 3.15, 3.17* and *3.18*) can be established in Greater Glasgow. This necessitates the study of neighbourhood, district and town centres as far as they exist and the extension, completion or generation of a conurbation-wide structure depending upon the degree to which provision centres do already exist. Once a complete potential structure is developed, the existing and newly required linkages between them will have to be investigated and established.

The main rules for the establishment of boundaries of areas – from neighbourhoods to towns – and their centres are based on the theoretical investigation of the city and city region's micro-structure:

• pedestrian scale for neighbourhoods and distances to centres of around 600 m so that people can walk to local services and facilities;

• four or five neighbourhoods to form a district and four or five districts to form a town;

Urban fabric

Industry

Neighbourhood boundaries

■   Existing neighbourhood provision centres

5–12. Existing and potential neighbourhood boundaries and centres in the conurbation of Glasgow (based on OS Pathfinder maps)

- a similar average gross population density in developed areas of around 60 persons per hectare to ensure the viability of services and facilities on all levels of the hierarchy of local, district, town and city centres.

If these rules could be translated from a theoretical model of a city or city region's micro-structure to a real city then the viability of the suggested urban structure would be confirmed and their importance for a more sustainable city or city region would be entrenched.

Existing Neighbourhood Centres and Real or Notional Neighbourhoods, Their Boundaries and Locations

Neighbourhood centres are recognisable through the location of post offices, police stations and, most of all,

primary schools. Therefore I have investigated the provision of schools in the Glasgow conurbation and mapped their location *(Fig. 5.11)*. The emerging picture shows a fairly clear and even distribution of schools throughout the conurbation. Schools are frequently located at the edge of neighbourhoods if there is insufficient space for the playing fields within the neighbourhood itself.

In the next stage an attempt is made to recognise the boundaries of neighbourhoods. The most important information is the location of schools. Then other features, especially edges – in the form of railway lines, major traffic routes, canals and rivers, linear green spaces, etc. – or breaks in the urban fabric help to draw boundaries around neighbourhoods *(Fig. 5.12)*. In some areas development is continuous and without a clearly establishable break in the urban fabric – specifically in the inner south-west/north-west development zone north of the river and west of the city centre up to

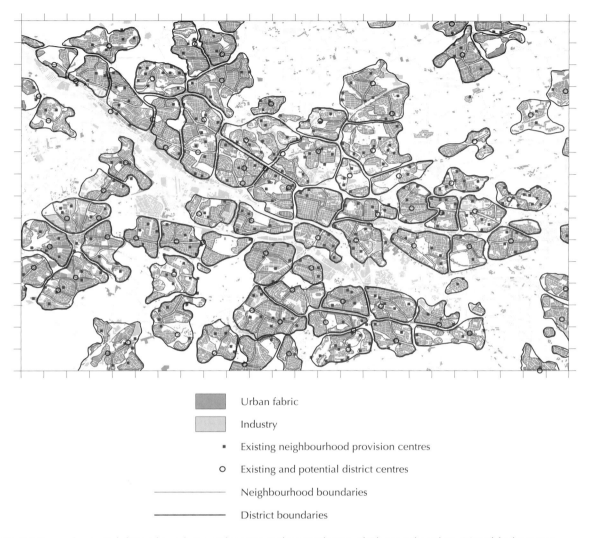

Urban fabric

Industry

■   Existing neighbourhood provision centres

○   Existing and potential district centres

——————   Neighbourhood boundaries

——————   District boundaries

5–13. Existing and potential district boundaries and centres in the conurbation of Glasgow (based on OS Pathfinder maps)

Clydebank (where a canal breaks the continuous development towards the west) and in the eastern part of the outer south-east/north-west development zone (around Rutherglen). In these areas boundaries of neighbourhoods are not so easily drawn, but additional information such as secondary transport routes or a change in the solid–void configuration or a change in the use pattern helps establish the more 'virtual' than real boundaries of neighbourhoods. When analysing the resulting neighbourhood pattern one can recognise that the size of their areas and their dimensions are generally similar. There are slight modifications to this regularity: in the more densely developed areas the neighbourhoods tend to be smaller in size, in garden suburbs and other development with much lower densities they tend to be larger. But overall, their dimen-

sions are fairly close to the demanded pedestrian scale with a radius of about 600 m, and both their demarcation and the location of their centres (notional or real) are mapped.

Real and Notional Districts and Their Centres

The established neighbourhood structure forms a very good base for the next stage of investigation, that of districts formed by a number of neighbourhoods. Again, natural breaks in the urban fabric and other features such as rivers, canals, major traffic routes and railway lines give an indication of the existing or potential grouping of, generally, four or five neighbourhoods around an existing or notional district centre *(Fig. 5.13)*. Where development is continuous – the West End and

	Urban fabric
	Industry
▪	Existing neighbourhood provision centres
○	Existing and proposed district centres
O	Existing 'town' (some in the form of retail parks)
○	Proposed new town centres
———	Neighbourhood boundaries
———	District boundaries
━━━	Town boundaries

5–14. Existing and potential town boundaries and centres in the conurbation of Glasgow (based on OS Pathfinder maps)

the outer East End – edges to districts are not always clearly establishable and in these cases the notional boundaries are represented with dotted lines; but in all these cases major traffic routes establish a kind of edge for or break between these districts.

For all districts centres are mapped which either exist or should exist in order to provide for a number of people services and facilities which are accessible by short public transport trips. Their location is, or is chosen to be, at crossing points of the major linkages between districts; this will guarantee their accessibility by a public transport network, which will be investigated later.

Real and Notional Towns and Their Centres

The pattern of districts and district centres leads to the next stage of investigation, that of towns and their centres. Generally four or five districts are grouped together to form towns, and town centres are located at major transport routes between towns *(Fig. 5.14)*. Again, in the more fragmented areas of the conurbation – specifically at its northern and southern edges – towns do already exist or potential ones can relatively easily be defined.

In the northern inner south-east/north-west development zone, and specifically in its western part, where development is more continuous, the boundaries of towns are more difficult to establish and potential town

▨	Urban fabric
▨	Industry
▪	Neighbourhood provision centres
○	District centres
◉	Existing 'town' centres
○	Proposed new town centres/river nodes
———	Primary linkages between town centres
———	Secondary linkages between district centres

5–15. Establishing linkages between existing and potential centres of provision in the conurbation of Glasgow (based on OS Pathfinder maps)

areas do overlap as one would expect. Again, as existing development and population densities in the western part of this zone are high, already well-established provision centres (distinguished in the map from notional ones) are closer together than in the less densely developed areas east, north and south of this zone.

The southern inner south-east/north-west zone is relatively shallow and sandwiched between the River Clyde and the M74 and M8 motorways south of the river. Accordingly the districts in this zone do not cluster to form towns and do not, therefore, have access to town centre facilities. This difficulty could have been avoided if the M74 and M8 motorways had been located further south, but a change of their location now, with most of the motorway stretches already built, would be unrealistic. The disadvantages that arise for the districts immediately south of the River Clyde will have to be taken into consideration when existing crossing points at the River Clyde and existing or potential river nodes are focused on. Overall, the investigation clearly indicates that a town structure does already exist to some extent and can relatively easily be extended over almost the entire area of the conurbation.

The city centre of Glasgow as defined by motorway and river represents a highly condensed central node of the size of a normal district dividable into four neighbourhoods. It does not form the centre of a town and lies therefore outside the town structure. The special role of the city centre in the conurbation is thus spatially and structurally reinforced.

Primary and Secondary Transport Networks Linking Neighbourhoods, Districts and Town Centres

Up to this point the application of a hierarchical micro-structure of development units and nodes in the conurbation of Glasgow has not caused any particular problems. Part of this structure is already there, albeit in rudimentary form. If all outlined neighbourhoods had the proposed average population density of 60 persons per hectare over 60% of their area, local services and facilities at their centre would be viable. Then neighbourhoods could form districts with a sufficiently high population density to afford district centre services and facilities, and districts could form towns with a sufficiently high population density to afford town centre services and facilities.

It goes without saying that provision centres of different capacities need to be accessible and the next stage of investigation needs to concentrate on transport networks. The exploration of neighbourhoods has already shown that the distance to neighbourhood centres from surrounding neighbourhood areas can be expected to be short, which makes it easy to walk or cycle from one's home or workplace to local services and facilities *(Fig. 5.12)*. An investigation of the actual configuration of the streets in neighbourhood areas and between neighbourhoods and district centres is therefore not necessary at this stage but will briefly be discussed in a number of cases in Chapter 6 in connection with the micro-structure of districts. Of major importance is, however, a transport network linking district centres with each other and district centres with town centres. With regard to these linkages the existing railway lines of the conurbation do not access the majority of district and town centres and, as already indicated, a light rail transit (LRT) system should be developed which would be placed in the streets and roads linking centres of provision.

When the placement of existing and potential district centres was being explored *(Fig. 5.13)*, locations at crossing points of roads linking with other districts were preferred. Therefore the network linking district centres with each other consists of existing roads which can easily be identified *(Fig. 5.15)*. Most of these roads are local distributors that do not, or should be redesigned not to, cater for through traffic. If necessary, the profile of these local distributor roads needs to be adjusted to

accommodate people, bicycles, public transport (e.g. buses) as well as local vehicular traffic in such a way that all users other than car drivers have priority over vehicular traffic. Bus lanes, cycle paths and traffic-calmed roads and streets might be the appropriate design solution. There are many publications (e.g. Richards, 1990; Moudon, 1987; Zuckermann, 1991; Gehl, 1987) which deal with street profiles that allow buses, cars, bicycles and pedestrians to use the same space safely; therefore no detailed suggestions of appropriate street profiles need to be worked out in this context.

Existing and proposed town centres are located at existing primary roads and road crossings and the network can easily be established. Some district centres are also located on such major roads or road crossings. There are two problems with the existing primary roads. First, they are major vehicular transport routes, often in the form of expressways and therefore excluding pedestrians and bicycles and largely excluding public transport (perhaps with the exception of buses). Second, west of the city centre at Central Station no level bridges cross the River Clyde. In the entire western stretch of the river there are only three crossings in total: the high-level bridge of the M8 motorway at the south-western edge of the city centre (Kingston Bridge), the Clyde Tunnel (linking Whiteinch with Govan) and the Erskine Bridge at the very north-western edge of the conurbation, again a high-level bridge (linking Old Kilpatrick with Erskine).

The first problem can be solved by redesigning the profiles of the primary roads to accommodate, next to the car, an inter-district and inter-town transport system, e.g. an LRT system, and bicycle routes as well as pavements for pedestrians; again priority of space use should be with public transport, not the car. The second problem can be solved by introducing a number of new bridges which establish new links between northern and southern towns and districts. At these new river crossings new activity nodes could be established which may have the status and scale of town centres but serve specific and city-wide purposes. Some of these river nodes already exist. There are, for instance, the bridges at Central Station, the area around which is presently derelict but could be developed into a major city centre attraction, for instance as a station for a super-fast train (the equivalent of the French TGV) linking Glasgow with Waterloo in London *(Fig. 5.16)*. Further west there is the Scottish Exhibition and Conference Centre with plans for a Science Centre, Millennium Tower, IMAX cinema as well as a Medium Park at Pacific Quay on the south side of the river *(The Courier, 1997, pp. 1–2)*. One other river node has been suggested but has not secured any funding yet: the proposed weir and inhabited bridge between Partick and Govan at the mouth of the River Kelvin, designed by Alsop *(Fig. 5.17)*. Several other

5–16. Railway and road bridges at Glasgow Central Station

nodes could be established at new bridge crossings further west, specifically between Yorker and Renfrew and, even further west, Clydebank and Erskine *(Fig. 5.15).* Each of the nodes could accommodate different city-wide activities, could be designed to be distinctive, and could contribute much to the revitalisation of the river valley west of the city centre. The river nodes could also generate a new city skyline, presently non-existent along the River Clyde, and this in turn would give the river a visual presence. In addition to revitalising the River Clyde, the nodes could also form much-needed links between communities on either side of the river. In and around these nodes new forms of high-density housing could be accommodated, benefiting from the

concentration of city-wide activities at the nodes, the high environmental quality of the river space and the beautiful vistas up and down the river and across to communities on either side. These nodes could also solve the problems with the districts south of the river, which do not cluster to form towns and have no immediate access to town centre services and facilities.

The areas in between the river nodes are part of the most important linear open space in the conurbation of Glasgow and could accommodate a large variety of functions from wildlife resort to recreation, forestry, farming, industry, culture and entertainment, larger-scale functions that do not easily fit into the smaller-grain urban fabric of districts and towns.

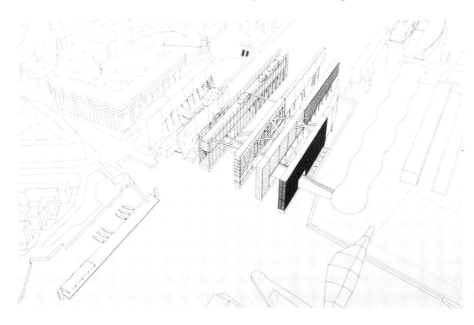

5–17. Inhabited bridge and weir linking Partick with Govan: scheme proposal by William Alsop of Alsop & Störmer Architects, London (reproduced with his kind permission)

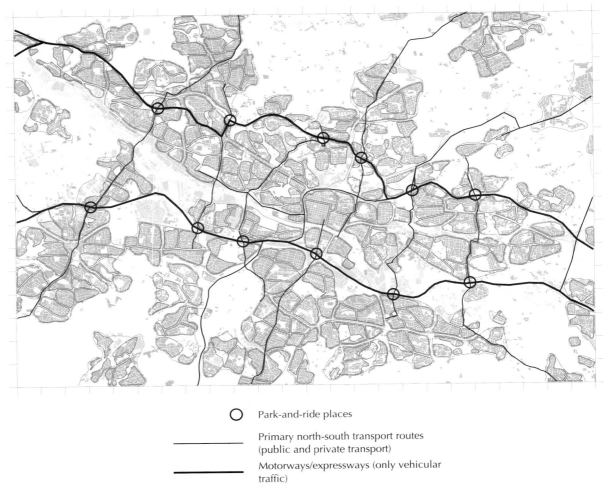

○   Park-and-ride places

_____   Primary north-south transport routes
(public and private transport)

▬▬▬▬   Motorways/expressways (only vehicular
traffic)

5–18. Proposed motorway system for Glasgow with alternative northern route and park-and-ride places (based on OS Pathfinder maps)

Primary Vehicular Transport Routes Bypassing Developed Areas and Centres

The primary and secondary transport network that links neighbourhoods, districts and towns and their respective centres having been established, just one problem remains, that of the major north-east/south-west vehicular traffic routes (motorways and expressways) north and south of the Clyde. As already mentioned, the routes allow access to urban areas from in between districts and allow through traffic to bypass built-up areas; but there is one exception: Great Western Road between the city centre and Anniesland Cross. This major traffic route passes through some of the most densely developed areas in Glasgow. As this stretch of the Great Western Road functions as a major vehicular traffic route as well as a retail street, congestion is considerable at particular times of the day (after rush hours, when parking

is permitted on either side of the road). To take non-local traffic out of this area, an alternative bypass further north needs to be found and the proposed route is located at gaps between districts of the inner and outer northern south-east/north-west development strips *(Fig. 5.18)*. With this modification all vehicular east–west through traffic would be located in open linear spaces between development clusters. At junctions of the south-east/north-west traffic routes – only for vehicular transport – with north/south traffic routes – all for both public and private transport, i.e. none for vehicular transport only except the north/south links at the very eastern and western edge of the conurbation – park-and-ride places could be established which would allow car drivers to change to public transport for access to towns, districts and neighbourhoods in the inner and outer northern and southern development zones. This arrangement

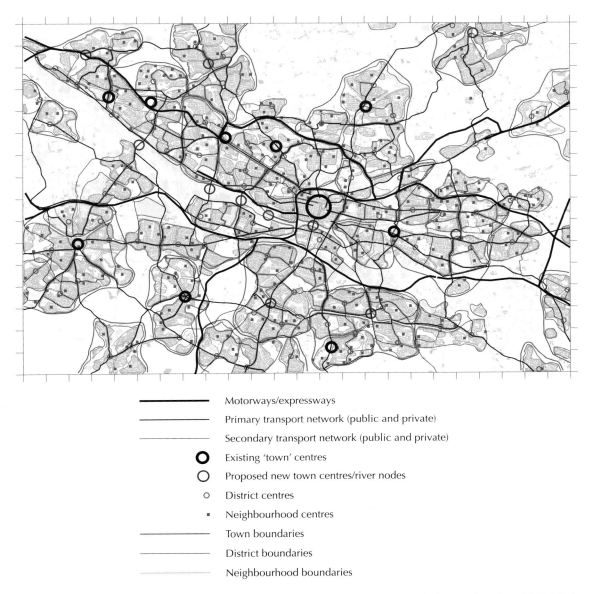

Legend	
▬▬▬▬▬	Motorways/expressways
─────	Primary transport network (public and private)
─────	Secondary transport network (public and private)
O	Existing 'town' centres
O	Proposed new town centres/river nodes
○	District centres
▪	Neighbourhood centres
─────	Town boundaries
─────	District boundaries
··········	Neighbourhood boundaries

5–19. Resulting hierarchical structure of provision centres and linkages in the conurbation of Glasgow (based on OS Pathfinder maps)

would greatly reduce the need to use the car inside built-up areas of the conurbation but would allow free vehicular traffic flow through the conurbation.

Conclusions

The investigation in this chapter has identified existing and potential neighbourhoods, districts and towns with their appropriate centres. It has demonstrated that a hierarchy of provision centres does already partially exist and could be expanded throughout the conurbation. Within this structure of development clusters and centres access to local, district and town centre services and facilities is fairly equal in all areas of the conurbation. It has also been demonstrated that a network of linkages between district centres and between these and town centres and the city centre also already exists but needs modification and expansion to allow public and private transport in parallel and to link areas north and south of the River Clyde west of the city centre with each other.

The resulting hierarchical structure of provisions centres and linkages *(Fig. 5.19)* follows closely the city model that seemed to be the most appropriate for the

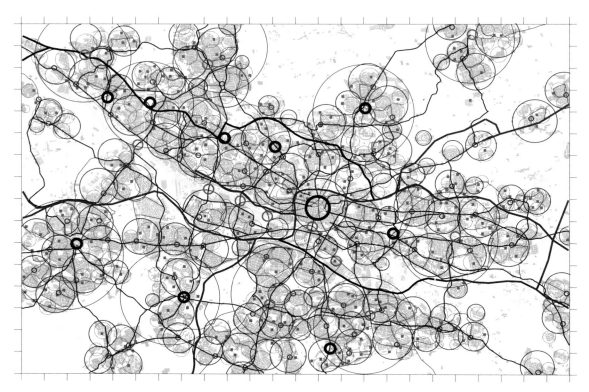

5–20. *Diagram of the structure of the conurbation of Glasgow over the figure-ground (based on OS Pathfinder maps)*

city region of Glasgow, the polycentric net. The proposed micro-structure of the conurbation is firmly based on the existing morphology and structure of Greater Glasgow and is therefore not only feasible but also achievable without any major structural changes to the city region and the conurbation.

5.4 Adaptability of the Structure to the Conurbation of Glasgow

It is now possible to abstract the proposed macro- and micro-structure for the conurbation of Glasgow in order to demonstrate how closely it resembles the abstract model of the polycentric net. The highlighting of all districts and towns (by circles with the appropriate radii), of the primary and secondary nodes (by dots of the appropriate visual weight) and of the primary and secondary transport links on the figure-ground base map *(Fig. 5.20)* illustrates that the structure is generated for, and follows closely, the existing pattern of development of the conurbation of Glasgow; but it is visually confusing. Therefore the base map with all details of the existing figure-ground is eliminated so as to show the city structure as a diagram *(Fig. 5.21)*. This diagrammatic representation of the city allows an immediate understanding of the polycentric nature of the conurbation and of the network of linkages between the nodes; it also demon-

strates how closely the real structure of the conurbation resembles the abstract pattern of the polycentric net.

The system of the polycentric net is open-ended and can adapt to any change in socio-economic conditions and can cope with any growth or shrinkage of population. In a real city this process is complex. If the population grows the question is which green areas should be developed; the decision does not involve major restructuring of an existing area and does not directly affect the existing population of districts or towns within the conurbation. Therefore expansion is relatively easy to manage. If, however, the population shrinks the question is whether, and if so which, built-up areas of the city could contract, and then existing communities will be directly affected.

One needs to remind oneself at this stage that the micro-structure will work efficiently only if all the centres are supported by the appropriate size of population, and this is currently not the case in all areas of the existing conurbation of Glasgow. Unfortunately data for the conurbation as a whole are not available; therefore this discussion concentrates on the city of Glasgow including Rutherglen (1975 boundaries). If 40% of the city area is allocated to open land (see section 3.3) and only 60% of the total area is built upon then the gross population density of Greater Glasgow is around 55.7 persons per hectare (pph) and therefore only a little short of

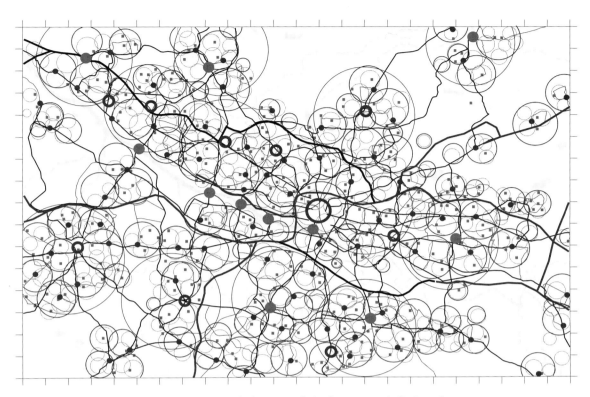

5–21. Diagram of the structure of the conurbation of Glasgow with the figure-ground eliminated

the 60 pph benchmark which is believed to be necessary to support local services and facilities and public transport. Glasgow's population is accordingly on average only a little too small, but it is rather unevenly distributed over the city area *(Fig. 4.32)*. Those districts with a population below the city average (with the 1975 boundary about 33.4 pph over the total area equivalent to a population of 55.7 pph over 60% of the area) represent 53.5% of the total city area but accommodate only 32% of the city's population *(Fig. 5.22)*. It is these

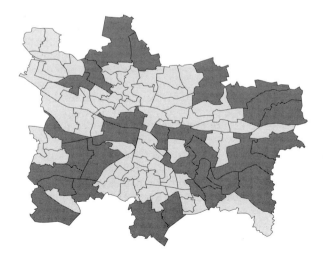

■ Areas of Glasgow (including Rutherglen) with population density below average

□ Area of Glasgow (including Rutherglen) with population at or above average

5–22. Areas in the city of Glasgow below the required average population density (based on Glasgow City Council, 1995)

districts that do not achieve a sufficient population to support local services and facilities. Many of them are located at the edge of the city and incorporate a considerable amount of open land over and above the 40% set as threshold value, but a number of them are located in the central development zone on either side of the River Clyde.

There is the additional problem of outmigration. The city population (excluding Rutherglen) fell from 1,055,000 in 1960 (Glasgow City Council, 1996, pp. 15–18) to 622,333 (Glasgow City Council, 1995) with only insignificant changes to the city boundary and area. This amounts to a population loss of 41% in that period. The decline was dramatic during the 1960s and 1970s, but during the 1980s and 1990s there was a steady decline in the rate of outmigration (between 1980 and 1993 around 3,000 persons or 0.5% a year with a falling tendency). Not to cope with the situation of uneven distribution and continued loss of the population would mean that the micro-structure would not work optimally in over half of the developed areas of the city. There are three ways of dealing with the mismatch between population and built-up area.

- Strategy one: increase the population in those areas with a population density below the city average (around 55.7 pph over 60% of the total area of Greater Glasgow). This strategy is based on the assumption that people could be attracted to move from the countryside or from the conurbation but outside the city into underpopulated areas of the city. With the proposed micro-structure the city population of Glasgow (including Rutherglen) would have to increase by 21.4% (145,226 people).

- Strategy two: increase the population in those areas below the threshold average by redistribution of population from areas with densities above average. This would require that 21.4% of the total city population living in districts with average and higher than average density would have to move into the 53.5% of the city's districts with densities below average.

- Strategy three: decrease the size of the built-up area of the city in those districts below the population average. This strategy is based on the assumption that the population in the higher-density area will or should not be reduced and that the population in the lower-density areas needs to be concentrated into a considerably smaller area to achieve the required gross density. This approach would involve demolition of existing fabric in and the dislocation of people out of 21.4% of the city area (4,348 ha).

Strategy One

The first strategy needs little further discussion as its advantages, but also its difficulties, are obvious. There is competition between urban districts and towns; some of those outside the city boundary of Glasgow offer better conditions for industry, services and other facilities to locate, and this causes outmigration. If competition could be changed into co-operation – clearly, the sustainability of individual places can be seen only in conjunction with the entire urban region – and if Glasgow could be made more attractive in terms of workplaces and general living conditions, then it might be possible to attract people into the city and achieve a more balanced population and workplace distribution in the conurbation and city region. This surely is the aim of many local agencies and departments but requires strategic plans for the regeneration of the entire region rather than individual areas in it.

Strategy Two

The second strategy considers that there may not be any need for an increase in the city's population or a decrease in the city's area if a more even distribution of population could be achieved in the individual built-up areas of the city. The problem with this strategy is that the weak areas of the city would be strengthened by weakening the strong areas, and this seems to be a problematic option. The densely populated neighbourhoods and districts are all historical areas of good spatial structure and form, and part of their quality is the high concentration of people which in turn supports good services and facilities. Quite apart from the fact that decanting population from the higher-density areas may reduce their quality and perhaps even viability, this strategy is likely to involve a considerable amount of restructuring of urban areas and dislocation of people and might therefore be economically and socially unacceptable.

Strategy Three

The third strategy has been widely, and often, discussed in Glasgow, causing considerable commotion at times. There have been suggestions that the city should get rid of the most deprived areas and relocate people from these areas into more advantaged districts. Others have suggested that areas at the very periphery of the city should be phased out and returned to farmland, regardless of their level of deprivation or otherwise, because they are furthest away from central services and facilities. It so happens that some of the most deprived areas are at the very edge of the city. Many of those who in recent decades have spent considerable sums of money and have made huge efforts to improve deprived areas – specifically the local housing associations and co-oper-

5–23. City of Glasgow: the most deprived areas (based on Glasgow City Council, 1995)

atives – have reacted strongly to such suggestions. They point out that there are communities and people in these areas who want to stay and further improve these districts. They also believe that demolition of housing stock and dislocation of people would only repeat the disasters of the comprehensive development of many urban areas immediately after the Second World War.

An examination of the location of the most deprived areas reveals that they are not only located at the very periphery of the city but also immediately north, east and south of the well-structured central belt *(Fig. 5.23)*. Therefore the level of deprivation on its own cannot be the basis for a decision to eliminate an urban area – if such a decision were ever to be made – because demolition frequently means shifting part of the problem elsewhere; the location of areas has to be considered as well.

It would make sense to start consolidation of the city in the more central areas because this would achieve more continuity of development with the appropriate structure and density right next to, and in good connection with, the already densely developed and well-structured city centre and the northern inner south-east/north-west development belt west of it. This would result in the priority regeneration of areas directly east, south and north of the city centre, and indeed one such project is already under way with the regeneration of the Crown Street area in the Gorbals, presently Glasgow's most coherent approach to the regeneration of a deprived area just south of the city centre, intended to bring people back into this inner-city zone. However, the regeneration of all urban areas in the city to the

same levels of quality and density as pursued in the Crown Street Regeneration Project might not be feasible unless the regeneration would entice more people and businesses to locate in the city. This reinforces the conviction that one strategy alone cannot solve all problems, and a combination of them may have to be applied.

Combination of Strategies

In reality all three strategies may well form part of a regeneration programme for the city and conurbation. All areas other than those that are already rather dense and well structured may undergo some form of compaction; some people and businesses may be attracted into the city because of added bonuses resulting from ongoing regeneration programmes; and some areas may be so derelict and so badly located that their regeneration into sustainable entities may prove too costly and thus they may actually be given up in favour of the regeneration of other, more promising areas.

A decision as to the right strategy needs to be based (a) on a thorough understanding of the qualities and deficiencies of all areas on the basis of the sustainability criteria already used earlier, and (b) on an assessment of the amount of restructuring required in each neighbourhood and district and the long-term costs and benefits of their restructuring. Regeneration of a district is in the end viable only if it can achieve within reasonable economic and social costs the required population density as well as affordable services and facilities and public transport, because only then will a district become a well-functioning and attractive part of a sustainable conurbation or city region. This in turn means that a decision to regenerate an individual district will have to be based (a) on the long-term costs and benefits of regeneration based on each of the three strategies, and (b) on the impact of the regeneration of a district on the entire conurbation and urban region.

5.5 Conclusions

The investigation of the city region and conurbation of Glasgow has generated evidence of the viability of the micro-structure of a more sustainable city. The investigation has also shown that for the region and conurbation of Glasgow the polycentric net is the most suitable macro-structure.

That Glasgow fits the polycentric net is, of course, no evidence of the general applicability of this macro-structure model of a city region. It happens to fit because of the specific development patterns as a result of specific topographical conditions of the city region, a unique historical development process and specific socio-economic conditions. Other city regions can be expected to have different features and may therefore demand the application of a different macro-structure model or even

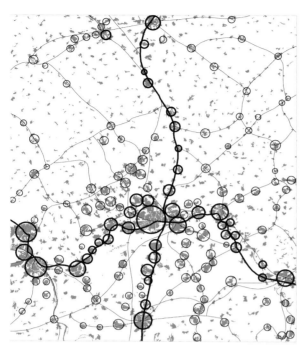

5–24. The macro-structure of the Rhine–Main region in Germany (based on Fig. 3.29 which is reproduced by kind permission of the Magistrate of the city of Frankfurt am Main)

a combination of different models.

The admittedly rather superficial return to the Rhine–Main region in Germany *(Fig. 5.24)* leads to the conclusion that in its centre (Frankfurt am Main) conditions may be similar to those in the Glasgow conurbation, albeit with a more compact inner area, specifically along the river, and more fragmented outer areas. But then this central area of the region is linked to rather fragmented development clusters, some of which form chains along transport routes. The overall structure of the region is still a kind of polycentric net but with two dominant linear development strips: a major east–west one along the rivers Rhine and Main (with Mainz/Wiesbaden to the west, Frankfurt in the middle and Aschaffenburg to the east) and a major north–south one in the centre of the region (with Darmstadt to the south, Frankfurt am Main in the middle and Wetzlar/Giesen to the north) (see Magistrat der Stadt Frankfurt am Main, 1997, p. 22; 1995, pp. 11, 15). The configuration of the Rhine–Main region is therefore a combination of net and linear development.

It appears therefore that the macro-structure of an individual town or city is in the end of relatively little significance when it comes to the definition of the form of a more readily sustainable conurbation or city region. It is the entire polycentric net that has to be taken into consideration; the existing conditions of such a net cannot be ignored, let alone easily changed. However, of considerable significance with regard to sustainability is the micro-structure of all parts of the net, which consists of a hierarchy of provision centres of different capacity (from neighbourhood to district to town and city centre) linked by a hierarchy of transport links of different capacity (from walkway and cycle path to motorway and from bus to LRT and railway). This structure provides not only access throughout the city, conurbation or region to a variety of services and facilities and to open land but also a high degree of mobility and in spatial and formal terms the potential for imageability of individual neighbourhoods, districts and towns.

A precondition for the viability of the micro-structure is a relatively modest degree of compactness of the development clusters (e.g. an average gross population density of around 60 persons per hectare throughout the city region). Compactness is not, however, required, and not even possible, in the city or city region at large, because of the inclusion of open land. It is needed in the individual neighbourhoods and districts and perhaps also towns that form the city or region.

This confirms what was concluded at the end of the evaluation of city models in Chapter 3. A city, conurbation or city region can have any of a variety of macro-structures and still score well with regard to sustainability criteria. Preconditions are that it has in all its parts the appropriate micro-structure and that extreme forms of compactness and concentration of population (in the form of a very large core city with a rather remote countryside) and extreme forms of decentralisation and dispersal of population (in the form of a galaxy of settlements or neighbourhoods) are avoided.

It has become clear in this investigation that the search for a generally valid sustainable city form is a bit of a red herring. What really counts is the search for a sustainable conurbation or city region. It has been demonstrated that in the region and conurbation of Glasgow a rudimentary micro-structure of the required nature does already exist and that this structure can be improved and expanded across the entire region without major upheaval and without major restructuring of the existing development pattern. What still requires investigation is how the micro-structure can be implemented in individual urban districts; this will be demonstrated with the help of a number of examples in Chapter 6.

References

The Courier, Bearsden, Milngavie & Glasgow West, (1997) Issue 553, Friday, 21 November.

Gehl, J. (1987) *Life between Buildings: Using Public Space,* Van Nostrand Reinhold, New York.

Glasgow City Council (1995) *Ward Profiles,* City Planning Department, Glasgow.

Glasgow City Council (1996) *Glasgow's Housing Plan 1996: Draft for Committee*, Housing Department, Glasgow.

Magistrat der Stadt Frankfurt am Main, Dezernat Planung, Amt für kommunale Gesamtentwicklung (1995) *Bericht zur Stadtentwicklung Frankfurt am Main 1995.*

Magistrat der Stadt Frankfurt am Main, Dezernat Planung, Amt für kommunale Gesamtentwicklung (1997) *Stadt-Pläne: Stadtentwicklungsplanung im Vergleich,* Internationaler Frankfurter Städtebau-Diskurs, Deutsches Architektur-Museum 29. Februar–1. März 1996.

Moudon, A.V. (ed.) (1987) *Public Streets for Public Use,* Van Nostrand Reinhold, New York.

Richards, B. (1990) *Transport in Cities,* Architecture Design and Technology Press, London.

Zuckermann, W. (1991) *End of the Road: The World Car Crisis and How We Can Solve It,* Lutterworth, Cambridge.

Strategic Design of Districts of the City of Glasgow

6

Having studied how a theoretical micro- and macro-structure of the city region can be applied in a real case, the city region and conurbation of Glasgow, and having seen how the concept of linked neighbourhoods, districts and towns can be implemented over the entire conurbation of that city, we still have to find out how the same micro-structure can be developed, or reinforced, in more detail in specific areas of that same city. For this exercise a number of districts with entirely different characteristics and problems have been selected. The question is whether one and the same structuring principle can be applied in all of them and what degree of transformation is needed in each of these districts.

This chapter first reiterates how city districts ought to be structured and what they ought to achieve. Then three different city areas (Bridgeton, Easterhouse and Partick/Govan) are investigated and a micro-structure of neighbourhoods is generated for the first two. The third case investigates the formation of a new river node. At the end of the chapter the required amount of change, new infrastructure and investment is compared with the potential benefits, and this in turn opens up a mechanism for decisions regarding the regeneration of areas over the entire conurbation and city region.

6.1 Objectives of, and Theoretical Framework for, the Structuring of Districts

Districts, and the neighbourhoods that form them, have been said to be the keystones of a conurbation and city region. It is useful to summarise again the specific properties such neighbourhoods and districts ought to have to achieve a more sustainable conurbation or city region:

- a reasonably high gross population density (about 60 persons per hectare) and with it a reasonable degree of compactness (in order to achieve viable neighbourhood and district centres, to reduce dis-

tances to supporting services and facilities and thus, to a degree, the traffic volume);

- a mixture of uses, in the neighbourhoods within walking distance, in districts accessible by short public transport rides (to increase access to services and facilities for those less mobile, reduce the need to travel, and achieve vibrant urban spaces and areas);

- a degree of social mix (to reduce or reverse social and locational stratification as a result of the population density and a variety of different dwelling and tenure types);

- public transport within districts (by bus) and between districts (by LRT) (to reduce car dependency and with it congestion, to increase mobility and choice throughout the conurbation or city region);

- traffic-calmed streets inside neighbourhoods and districts, park-and-ride places at inter-district routes between districts (to reduce the volume and speed of vehicular traffic inside built-up areas);

- a clear and lasting identity and image for individual neighbourhoods and districts (which can be established through a specific mixture of uses, through memorable nodes, linkages and markers which generate places with lasting image, perhaps in some cases through the clustering of urban fabric);

- an adaptable urban fabric (with the exception of those elements generating a lasting image, to allow development to adapt to changing socio-economic needs) and a degree of autonomy for the communities so that they can decide their own appropriate development form;

- good access to open countryside (for recreation and sports but also to establish a degree of self-sufficiency for neighbourhoods and districts as a result of entrepreneurial activities).

The following investigation will not discuss details of the development of urban areas but remain on the level of strategic decisions and frameworks and study specifically the spatial and organisational structure of neighbourhoods and districts that help achieve the desired properties.

The major spatial and structural features of a sustainable micro-structure discussed in section 3.1 all had to do with pedestrian access to neighbourhood centres (e.g. a maximum distance from the edge of a neighbourhood to its centre of about 600 m) and short public transport rides from the neighbourhood centres to district centres (e.g. a distance of 1,300–1,450 m between edge and centre of a district consisting of four to five neighbourhoods and having a core area with a radius of about 150 m) (*Figures 3.02* and *3.08*). The investigation in principle of the existing neighbourhood provision centres in Glasgow and of existing or potential boundaries of neighbourhoods and districts has established that in most areas neighbourhoods cluster to form districts, but that in some areas the depth of development is insufficient to allow the formation of a district centre. The question is, therefore, how the micro-structure can be implemented and, if necessary, adapted to the local conditions of individual districts.

6.2 Case Studies of the Transformation of Districts in the City of Glasgow

For the purpose of demonstrating the applicability of the micro-structure in urban districts urban areas have been selected in different parts of the city. They each have a different history of development, have different properties and deficiencies and therefore have different problems and may therefore require a different approach. The selected districts are Bridgeton to the south-east of the city centre, Easterhouse at the eastern fringe of the conurbation, and the river area between Partick and Govan west of the city centre *(Fig. 6.01)*.

Bridgeton

The selected area has Bridgeton at its centre but includes Calton to the west and Camlachie to the east. Its immediate neighbours are Dennistoun to the north, separated by a linear belt of open and industrial land; Parkhead to the east, separated from Bridgeton by a cemetery (Eastern Necropolis); Dalmarnock to the south-east and south, separated by a defunct railway line and by industry; and Glasgow Green to the south-west. Bridgeton is accordingly well linked with, but spatially separated from, other urban districts, with the exception of a continuous link with the city centre via Calton, but its boundaries are frequently unclear and need to be reviewed *(Fig. 6.02)*.

This district was once a burgh in its own right, with a market cross at the centre which still shows the radial pattern of streets linking it with its surroundings. The burgh was amalgamated into the city boundary and expanded into a densely developed urban district with an intense mixture of industry and tenement housing. Development of individual areas of the district is based on a kind of grid structure which frequently changes orientation in order to fit into the radial pattern of the main streets. The market cross and the radial routes linking it to other areas establish a clear centre for the

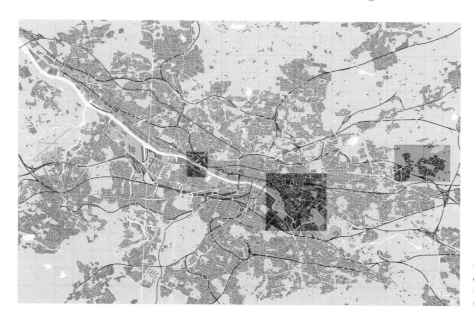

6–01. Districts to be investigated and their location in the Glasgow conurbation (based on OS Pathfinder maps)

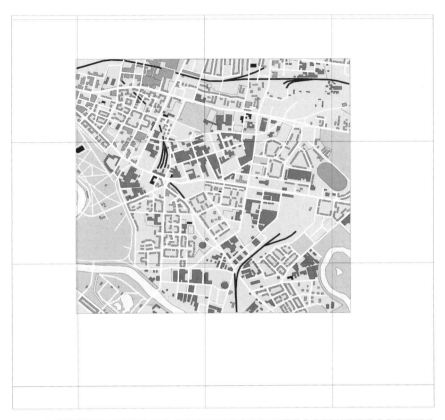

6–02. *Figure-ground showing the existing development pattern of the Bridgeton district (based on OS Pathfinder maps)*

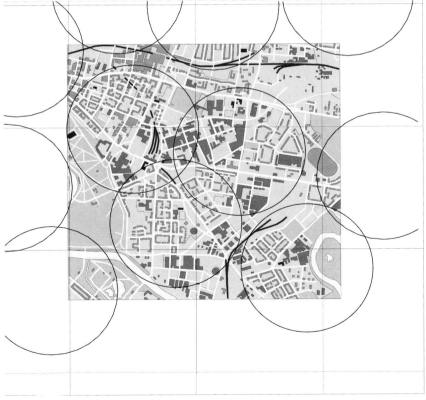

6–03. *Figure-ground of Bridgeton with potential neighbourhoods highlighted (based on OS Pathfinder maps)*

Open space

Urban fabric

Mixed-use development peaks at neighbourhood and district centres

● Marker

○ Centres in adjacent districts/neighbourhoods

━━━━ Secondary transport routes

━━━━ Local transport links

6–04. Design framework for the Bridgeton district (based on OS Pathfinder maps)

district, but this centre suffers from a high volume of through traffic. There are no obvious secondary or neighbourhood centres. Owing to the decline of traditional industry the area suffers today from a considerable degree of dilapidation and fragmentation of its urban fabric. In addition, Bridgeton is one of the most deprived areas of the city and suffers specifically from a high degree of unemployment. Considering the entire district (i.e. including Calton, Bridgeton and Dalmarnock) the percentage of unemployed against the figure of those in or potentially in employment is 16.3% against a city average of 9.8% (Glasgow City Council, 1995).

There is accordingly a strong spatial structure of a main centre, radial primary routes converging at Bridgeton Cross, and a secondary grid of local streets and urban blocks. The central space is located some-

what off-centre of the area but distances to the edges from the centre are only around 1,000 m or even less. The development patterns in the chosen area vary considerably, and three different neighbourhoods can easily be detected: Calton to the north-west and towards the city centre with an irregular grid and reasonably sized blocks; the area north-east of the cross, again with an irregular grid but with large impermeable blocks of industry (predominant use) and sports fields; and the area south-east of the cross (towards Dalmarnock) in which the grid structure is somewhat erratic and in places interrupted by large impermeable blocks *(Fig. 6.03)*. The scale of these neighbourhoods is close to that required but, with a radius of around 500 m, on the small side. However, as major green spaces are, or are potentially, available in very close proximity to the neighbourhoods, larger open spaces can be provided at

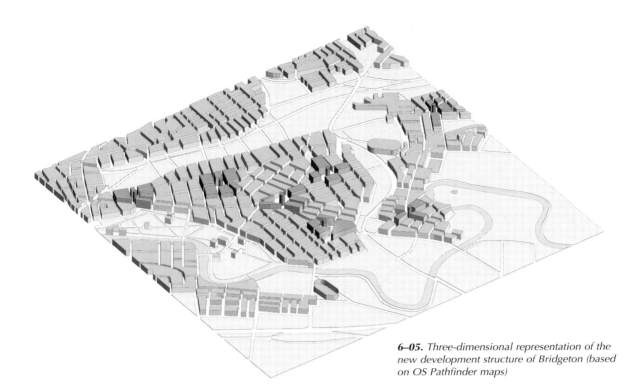

6–05. Three-dimensional representation of the new development structure of Bridgeton (based on OS Pathfinder maps)

the edge of rather than inside the district, and this will help achieve the required population density.

In design terms the main problems of the area are:

- the degree of dilapidation of the urban fabric; the out-of-character and out-of-scale development in Calton during the 1970s and 1980s in the then GEAR (Glasgow East Area Renewal) area;

- through traffic, specifically through Bridgeton Cross;

- some large-scale city blocks which considerably reduce permeability;

- unclear definition of the edge of the district specifically to the north, east and south (predominantly industrial areas).

The design concept for the district *(Fig. 6.04)* attempts to solve the edge problems of the district by incorporating the spaces north, east and west of the district into linear open north–south and east–west spaces. This equates to a decrease in the built-up area, which becomes more compact; the freed areas, now clearly part of a linear open space system, can accommodate larger-scale functions such as industrial and sports facilities which presently intersect finer-grain development. The larger-scale urban blocks are split to ease development and improve permeability; this requires a modest increase of streets and infrastructure.

The three neighbourhoods already identified overlap with each other but a clear central space with local services and facilities can be established for each of them (as well as other central spaces of surrounding neighbourhoods). They occupy roughly 350 ha (excluding the open linear spaces) and could accommodate approximately 18,000–21,000 people. A number of street links between the neighbourhood centres and the district centre are highlighted and between these and other neighbourhood centres in the vicinity. These streets are predominantly for public transport, and pedestrian use and vehicular traffic is slowed down on these streets as well as on all local streets inside the neighbourhoods.

The framework demonstrates that the micro-structure with the required centres of provision and linkages can be established with relatively modest effort by exploiting and reinforcing the existing development pattern. There are no major changes to the pattern except that some of the larger-scale functions have been shifted into the linear open spaces surrounding part of the district (not illustrated). The area to the north-east of the district, which presently accommodates an out-of-town retail park, might be transformed into a town centre at the heart of several other districts to its north, east and south as already indicated in Chapter 5 *(Fig. 5.19).* A whole range of provision centres is therefore possible as long as the required population density can be achieved.

The three-dimensional representation of the new development structure illustrates the even density of

(a)   *(b)*

6–06. *Comparison of existing and proposed development pattern of the Bridgeton district. (a) Existing pattern; (b) proposed pattern*

urban fabric with higher peaks at and around the neighbourhood and district centres with a high concentration of mixed uses *(Fig. 6.05)*. The centres also accommodate a marker that gives the neighbourhoods as well as the district identity and a sense of centrality.

A comparison between the existing city block and road pattern and that of the proposed design framework shows that most of the road infrastructure exists and only relatively minor additions are required to achieve the new pattern of neighbourhoods and district *(Fig. 6.06)*.

Easterhouse

The second district to be investigated, Easterhouse, is one of the peripheral estates. It is located north of the M8 motorway at the very north-eastern edge of the city. The plan of the district's current condition (mid-1980s) *(Fig. 6.07)* shows a very loose development which includes a large amount of open land, most of it green, some hard-landscaped, almost all of it without proper function. Another feature is the exaggerated scale of the blocks, many of which include far too large courtyards which accordingly are hardly usable. Therefore the overall density is rather low despite the original

6–07. *Figure-ground showing the existing development pattern of Easterhouse (based on OS Pathfinder maps)*

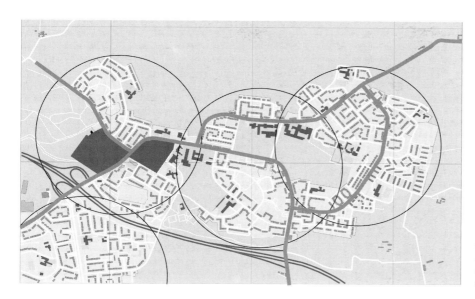

6–08. Figure-ground of Easterhouse with potential neighbourhoods highlighted (based on OS Pathfinder maps)

use of four-storey tenement blocks, which in traditional development achieve high densities. If the admittedly large amount of surrounding farmland is eliminated, the gross population density can be expected to be around 40 persons per hectare (pph), a density close to that achieved by areas which are predominantly developed as garden suburbs (like, for instance, Knightswood with around 49 pph *(Fig. 4.10)*). This highlights the major problem of this district: a poor spatial structure and a somewhat low population density despite concentration of population in high-density dwelling blocks. Easterhouse is also one of the deprived city areas with an

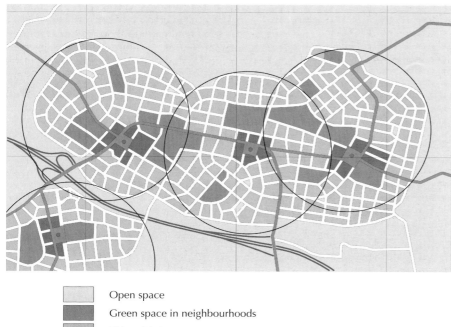

Open space
Green space in neighbourhoods
Urban fabric
Mixed use development peaks at neighbourhood centres
● Marker
Local transport links

6–09. Design framework for Easterhouse (based on OS Pathfinder maps)

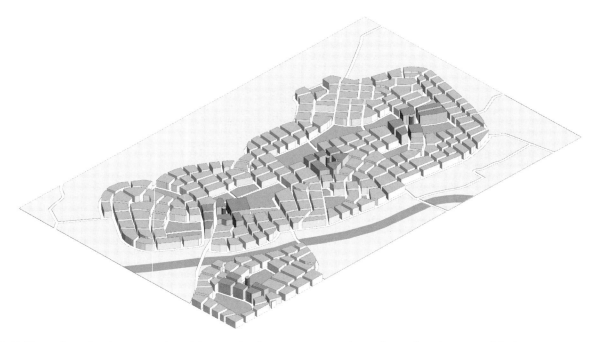

6–10. *Three-dimensional representation of the new development structure of Easterhouse (based on OS Pathfinder maps)*

unemployment rate of 17.1% against a city average of 9.8% (again calculated against the figure of employed or potentially employed people) (Glasgow City Council, 1995).

The area north of the M8 on which this investigation focuses is clearly fragmented by green open spaces into three areas of the scale of what could develop into neighbourhoods *(Fig. 6.08)*. Each of these areas seems to have school provision and there is the occasional post office, but the only existing shopping centre and all major community facilities are located in the western neighbourhood area. The distance to this centre from the eastern neighbourhood area is close to 2,000 m and therefore easily reachable only by bicycle, car or bus.

In design terms the main problems of the area are as follows:

- even if the large green open spaces surrounding Easterhouse are disregarded, the population density is on the low side (according to Glasgow City Council (1995), 18,739; with three full-size neighbourhoods one would expect about 21,000 people); however, as population is concentrated in tenement blocks current regeneration plans tend to reduce the number of floors or replace the tenements altogether with terraced family houses; this in turn will result in a gradual reduction of population which in turn will reduce the viability of community services and facilities;

- many of the open spaces inside the district have no specific function and represent barriers between built-up areas; as a result permeability is rather poor;

- the urban block sizes are almost all far too large and need to be broken up or otherwise reduced;

- traffic is concentrated onto a major access route which forms an extensive loop through housing areas;

- services and facilities other than schools are concentrated in the western neighbourhood; the central and eastern neighbourhoods have no provision centre;

- the edges of the district to the country are arbitrary and need to be reviewed.

The design concept for the district *(Fig. 6.09)* attempts to generate clear centres for all three neighbourhoods, which are linked with each other by a new central route. This route would accommodate the major public transport line linking the area with the city centre. To achieve this, the large internal green areas have been reduced in size to generate more development along the central route, which would accommodate, next to new housing, community facilities specifically at and around the centres of the neighbourhood, i.e. within walking distance of their edges. The urban block sizes have been

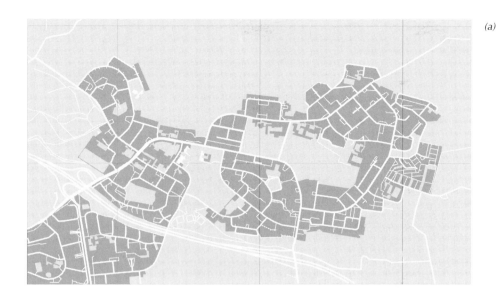

(a)

(b)

6–11. Comparison of existing and proposed development pattern of Easterhouse. (a) Existing pattern; (b) proposed pattern

reduced throughout to increase the density of development with low-rise dwelling types, and achieve a more even distribution of the population and a higher degree of permeability. Additional areas at the periphery of the neighbourhoods have been developed to improve the borders with the countryside and also to increase the population to the neighbourhoods' full potential without an undue concentration of people.

The three-dimensional representation of the new development structure shows an even density of development with peaks at the neighbourhood centres which accommodate mixed use and a marker to give each neighbourhood an identity and a sense of centrality (Fig. 6.10).

The configuration now achieved, which is based on

the main characteristics of the existing development pattern, represents a considerable improvement in terms of density (which is more evenly spread), compactness (through the reduction of unnecessary open spaces in the neighbourhoods) and local centres of provision. However, the linearity of development at the edge of the city prevents the clustering of neighbourhoods around a district centre. In contrast to the first example of Bridgeton – where a clear district centre is already in existence and where the spatial structure is fairly good and needs only to be improved – Easterhouse will not achieve a natural district centre without a considerable amount of new development or restructuring. In addition to the lack of centrality, the amount of restructuring of urban blocks is considerable and the required

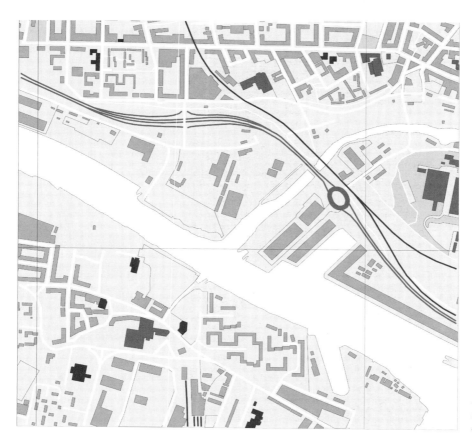

6–12. *Figure-ground showing the existing development patterns of the river area between Partick and Govan*

expansion of roads and infrastructure vast *(Fig. 6.11)*. However, without the new spatial structure the neighbourhoods would not work nearly as well as they should. The question arises therefore whether the huge efforts are worth the limited benefits that are achieved or whether even more efforts should be undertaken in the form of the construction of additional neighbourhoods to form a proper district with central facilities.

A Link between Partick and Govan

The third case study is not one of a single district but focuses on one of the potential new river crossings and nodes between two communities, Partick north of the Clyde and Govan south of it *(Fig. 6.12)*. Partick has a clear tenement block structure north of Dumbarton Road, but this structure disintegrates towards the rivers Kelvin and Clyde. Govan has lost almost all of its historical pattern, and in particular the area around Govan Cross is largely dilapidated. Different housing schemes and disused industry float in lost space.

In design terms the main problems of the area are:

- the lack of a link across the river (there was once a ferry but now there is no direct link at all; connections are possible only via Kingston Bridge,

the city centre or the road tunnel further west in Govan); without a bridge the river is a barrier;

- the development of Partick towards the rivers is dilapidated and needs a new structure;

- an above-ground railway line and an expressway cut the tenement area of Partick off from the river zone;

- Partick Cross at the junction of Dumbarton Road and Byres Road has lost its enclosure and definition;

- Govan Cross needs a new enclosure and the entire area towards the river and the south a new spatial structure.

The design concept for the new river crossing and the edges of both communities *(Fig. 6.13)* suggests an expansion of the development pattern at Dumbarton Road down to the rivers Kelvin and Clyde. A new road is introduced which links Partick Cross via the river node and bridge to Govan Cross and from there further south. This route is largely green (with the exception of the area around Govan Cross) and establishes an open-space link from Kelvingrove Park via Govan potentially to Bellahouston Park and Pollok Park to the south

Open/green space

Urban fabric

Mixed-use development peaks at Partick Cross (north) and
Govan Cross (south)

● Marker

Local transport links

*6–13. Design framework for the
river area between Partick and
Govan (based on OS Pathfinder
maps)*

(beyond the map). The green space would link and
could extend cultural facilities already available in Kelvingrove Park and Bellahouston Park. For the Govan
area a new block structure is developed which is largely
based on the existing infrastructure.

The major achievement of such a design concept is
not only the repair of the structure of both communities
on either side of the River Clyde – a process similar to
that demonstrated for Bridgeton and Easterhouse – but
that the communities develop a front towards the river
and are linked by a new bridge. The three-dimensional
representation of the new structure and river node
shows the improved block pattern and its extension
towards the rivers, the new linkage and markers for
Partick and Govan Cross *(Fig. 6.14)*. Many schemes of a
similar kind have been developed in recent years for the
Partick–Govan area, including one by the author in
1990 for an international conference *(Fig. 6.15)*. The

latest project, a scheme by Will Alsop, which develops
the river node into an inhabited bridge and weir, has
already been introduced in Chapter 5 *(Fig. 5.17)*.

6.3 Conclusions

The case studies clearly demonstrate that there are considerable differences in existing qualities and deficiencies of individual districts in the conurbation of
Glasgow. In some cases (like Bridgeton, a deprived area)
the existing structure is good and needs little change
and addition to generate neighbourhoods with their
centres located around a district centre. In other cases
(like Easterhouse, also a deprived area) the required
amount of restructuring and extension of the existing
infrastructure would have to be considerable merely to
establish a neighbourhood structure, and even more
extensive if a proper district were to be formed.

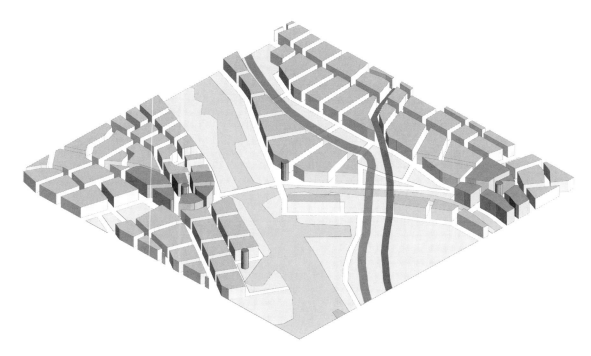

6–14. *Three-dimensional representation of the new development structure of the area between Partick and Govan (based on OS Pathfinder maps)*

6–15. *Model of a previous scheme developed by the author for the Urban Edges Conference in Glasgow, 1990*

The insight into the required amount of restructuring and the benefits resulting from it is a useful basis for the decision regarding a regeneration programme for the entire conurbation. When the considerably reduced population level of Glasgow, discussed in section 5.4, is taken into account, a decision to apply one or a combination of the three strategies in each specific district would be possible on the basis of an understanding of the costs involved and the long-term benefits achievable. This in turn could help a decision as to which areas to develop and which other areas in the city to return to farmland or other open-space uses should it not be possible to increase the population level considerably.

However, the consideration of costs and benefits on its own is not sufficient. It is vital that the social conditions in districts and neighbourhoods are taken into account and that the communities are involved in the decision-making process and therefore support resolutions regarding the future of their areas. Furthermore, the location of each individual district in the conurbation and its role within the polycentric net need to be taken into consideration as well. In some cases the restructuring may have to be carried out no matter what efforts are required because of the importance of certain districts for the continuity of the net or because of the location of a district close to the major centre of the net or because of the historical importance of a district or because of the strength of particular communities. In other cases even modest restructuring efforts may prove not to be justifiable because of the isolated location of a district at the edge of the conurbation or because the achievable improvement is insufficient as a consequence of the poor existing structure and form of a district.

References

Glasgow City Council (1995) *Ward Profiles*, City Planning Department, Glasgow.

Epilogue

It is generally accepted that our cities have to be made to function better and to become more people-friendly, that their destructive environmental impact has to be reduced and that the countryside needs to be protected from further urban sprawl. It is also generally accepted that the very form and structure of our cities need to be improved in order to achieve these objectives, and this clearly calls for strategic plans and design frameworks. It seems to be evident that such design frameworks are urgently needed at city region, city and city district level. The question to be addressed now is how to generate such frameworks. This book demonstrates an approach based on what are believed to be commonly agreed sustainability criteria, but in the real world of urban regeneration it might be difficult to achieve consensus on such a set of criteria – and, perhaps even more importantly, how to implement them.

A Slow and Incremental Process of Transformation

Despite the urgency of change it should not happen in a compressed span of time. The approach must be gentle rather than radical and any transformation process must be slow, incremental and carried by the people. The transformation must also be feasible. Wholesale demolition and new build is not the way to do it again; it is neither economically viable nor socially acceptable. The results of comprehensive development during the 1950s and 1960s are still all too obvious and depressing. Instead, the normal process of development and change of the city, at its normal speed, must be directed by strategic planning and design frameworks in such a way that incremental development projects will slowly but steadily achieve a better-functioning, socio-economically more balanced and more user- and environment-friendly city. Improvement must occur through 'conservative surgery' as Geddes calls his approach to urban renewal (see Meller, 1981, pp. 54–6).

In an incremental process of regeneration, individual urban areas can undergo change with little effect on other districts. In terms of activities, some cease, others continue and yet others start up without threatening the economic and social viability of the city at large as long as there is a wide range of activities of different scale and importance. Development projects must occur within the normal process of city renewal and change. However, in contrast to what generally happens today, they must all be co-ordinated and integrated by design framework of the city region and the city districts in order to achieve steady improvement through concerted actions. For this to be achieved there must be a commonly accepted concept of a sustainable city region and a shared list of the main properties it ought to have. In view of the confusion engendered by the current debate on a sustainable city, such a common concept might be difficult to develop, let alone to accept, despite the fact that it is urgently needed.

The Need for Flexible Regeneration Frameworks

Socio-economic conditions change. Therefore regeneration frameworks can afford to be rigid only in their principles and must remain flexible and open-ended in their details. The change of the urban fabric of a district, town or city, and with it of the macro-structure of a city region, is not predictable over a long period of time, neither is the use pattern of individual spaces in individual districts and towns of that region. In contrast, basic human needs do not change dramatically even over a longer period of time. Access to centres of provision with services and facilities of a different capacity and for different catchment areas can therefore be considered to be a fairly constant demand. Access to the open country can also be classified as a stable requirement. Mobility too is a constant and ever more important requirement in a city and city region, and it should be facilitated without environmental degradation and without congestion.

Long-term frameworks should focus on these stable demands on a city and city region and develop the support structure with a hierarchy of provision centres linked by a hierarchy of transport systems. This structure can be considered to develop incrementally but then to remain relatively stable, at least in its main elements of nodes and linkages. Rather than focusing on use patterns as today's structure plans frequently do, development frameworks should concentrate on the nodal and transport structure which allows use patterns to develop and modify.

The Need for Political Support for Long-term Strategic Plans

The problem with the slow and incremental process of the city's regeneration is not an economic one; it does not necessarily require larger sums of money than are spent anyway. The problem is that it requires that the money is spent at the right time in the right place. This in turn necessitates the orchestration and co-ordination of development projects over a long period of time, maybe 50 or more years, to get somewhere close to a more sustainable structure for the city and city region. Such co-ordination and orchestration calls for long-term strategies and development frameworks the basic principles of which are adhered to over the entire period of regeneration and by everybody involved in the regeneration process, from politicians and professionals to members of the individual communities.

In a planning system that has adjusted to the short-termism of politics and operates with departments that frequently compete rather than collaborate with each other, this seems to be impossible. There seems also to be a lack of political will at present to start such a long-term regeneration process because it might make things difficult and, more likely, because it might infringe upon the liberty of economic forces shaping today's cities and become counter-productive. However, without some form of long-term co-operation of all those involved in city development – be it developers and investors, politicians and professionals, or be it the citizens themselves – a more sustainable city region is not achievable. The long-term and incremental regeneration programme calls for, and is dependent upon, strong political leadership and a strong political will to adhere to the programme's principles over a very long period of time. It is also essential that a co-ordinated approach and local action be supported rather than prevented by plans at regional or national level; this calls for co-ordinated policies. Without political leadership and determination and without co-ordinated policies – exemplified in cities like Barcelona – little will in the end be achieved despite all ongoing efforts and all investment.

The Need for Regional rather than Local Thinking, Planning and Design

If all sustainability criteria are taken into consideration it becomes clear that the city on its own cannot ever be sustainable because it depends on its regional and even global environment, with which it should have a balanced, non-exploitational and non-destructive relationship. Therefore planning and design frameworks for individual cities within their existing political boundaries are totally inept and actually counter-productive; frequently urban development does not recognise such political boundaries but has a regional structure, as the study of the conurbation of Glasgow has exemplified. What is required is the rethinking of the boundaries of planning and design areas, and these areas should be defined not by political whim but on the basis of the functional, socio-economic, environmental, geographic and cultural interrelatedness and interdependence of urban areas within a regional context. Furthermore, planning and design frameworks need to be established on a number of levels – from the national to the regional, local and space specific – and this necessitates the establishment of planning and design bodies that operate co-operatively rather than competitively on these levels.

It is interesting that in 1996, through intervention of the Scottish Office, a 'Glasgow and the Clyde Valley Structure Plan Joint Committee' was set up with the task to generate a development strategy for the Glasgow and Clyde Valley metropolitan area (information obtained from the Joint Committee, Glasgow). The plan area is, and necessarily so, even wider than the one considered as the 'Glasgow region' in section 5.1 and reaches from Inverclyde and West Dumbartonshire to South Lanarkshire.

The key objectives for the new structure plan are said to be a sustainable development strategy, economic regeneration, social equity, environmental quality, integration of land use and transportation. These objectives play an important role in the debate on a sustainable structure for the city and city region (see Chapter 2) and have influenced the discussion of their micro- and macro-structure (see Chapter 3). The key strategic planning issues are said to be urban regeneration and renewal, economic development, integrated transportation policies, greenbelt protection and enhancement, sustaining the city and town centres, housing demand and supply, retail development, and conservation of the environment and heritage of the area.

It seems that the co-ordination of local development with the help of a development framework for the entire metropolitan area is a good step forward in a process of achieving a sustainable urban region. It is essential, however, that an appropriate concept of a sustainable city region exists as a stable and long-lasting base for such a framework.

The Need for Community Involvement in Urban Regeneration

Much of the recent urban development and regeneration, specifically post-war comprehensive development, was dictated by professionals and politicians. Much of it today occurs with little co-ordination as a result of the actions of competitive economic forces which do not seem to have a particular interest in a specific city or city region. It is most important that the process of urban development and regeneration be freed from mere economic exploitation, become apolitical and involve people and communities actively so that they can influence development in response to their needs and aspirations. Geddes' approach of 'conservative surgery', already mentioned, involves the active participation of the inhabitants. This in turn enables them, as he puts it, to identify with their places and, by their involvement in the city improvement process, themselves to undergo a process of individual development and learning (see Meller, 1981, p. 56).

Participation in the process of shaping the city and city region is possible only if those currently claiming to have the right and the professional skills and administrative responsibility to control urban development surrender their autocratic position and allow people and communities to get involved. Participation is difficult at a regional and even at a city level and when it comes to frameworks for a metropolitan area, but the creation of neighbourhoods and districts facilitates the involvement of communities in the shaping of their own areas.

The Need to Analyse the Impact of Individual Regeneration Projects

A slow, incremental approach to the restructuring and regeneration of the city and city region has the considerable advantage that it allows the impact of individual actions to be monitored and lessons to be learned for subsequent actions. It is essential that the monitoring of the functional, social, economic and environmental consequences of individual development projects in neighbourhoods, districts, towns, the city and the city region becomes a standard component of the urban regeneration process and approach. Regular audits ought to assess what has been achieved and what has not or not yet been achieved, whether the more constant and long-lasting concepts of the underlying strategy have been adhered to in full, whether the strategy succeeds in achieving what it has promised to achieve and whether it may have to be adapted or expanded. City regeneration ought to be based on the long-term assessment of costs and benefits achievable by strategic frameworks, and individual decisions and projects ought to be checked with regard to the degree to which they achieve the predicted benefits within the cost framework. Only with the help of such constant monitoring can the frameworks achieve in the end a more sustainable relationship of the city with its hinterland, a more people-friendly and socio-economically balanced city.

The Need to Review Professional Responsibilities and Education

Involving people in the process of urban regeneration and development requires a different professional approach from that generally applied at present. The planning and design process has to become transparent and planners and designers have to listen not only to developers and investors but also to the people in order to achieve a balance of demands on the city and city region.

Professionals also have to recognise that dealing with the city region is dealing with physical reality, a spatial and volumetric entity which has to be structured and formed to work efficiently and economically; and this means that anyone involved in the process of urban regeneration and development has to understand and has to be able to deal with the structural, spatial and formal nature of the urban environment.

Professionals with different expertise should start working together in multi-disciplinary teams so that the knowledge and skills of all of them help shape the form and structure of a city region in all its components. Comprehensive solutions towards a sustainable urban structure need to respond to all functional, social, economic, environmental and ecological demands on the city environment and cannot, therefore, be developed with a series of isolated single-aspect planning and design acts.

To enable professionals to understand each other and to be able to collaborate necessitates the review not only of professional practice but of professional education. The categorical divide between architecture and planning in the UK and elsewhere – which some try to solve by creating yet another discipline, urban design – needs to be overcome rather than patched up; both should at least have common educational routes, and these routes should generate the ability of all to understand the city as a complex spatial, formal, structural and environmental entity. As was stated at the beginning of this book, design is, or ought to be, a component of all disciplines involved in the shaping and reshaping of the city. Therefore education programmes for all these disciplines ought to incorporate a strong design base unless, in an even more radical approach, all relevant disciplines are amalgamated into one single one which provides a common and design-based foundation for all and allows specialisation on top of it.

Conclusions

It is becoming evident that to achieve sustainable city regions requires the rethinking not only of the city and city region but also of current policies, approaches and professional responsibilities as well as education. What is needed is a strong commitment to the city and its hinterland, a strong political will to act upon this commitment by implementing strong, co-ordinated policies, approaches and strategies; and this equates with a kind of gentle and friendly revolution. Half-heartedness will not achieve sustainable city regions. Let us hope that there is enough time left to achieve effective change.

References

Glasgow and the Clyde Valley Structure Plan Joint Committee (no date) *A New Plan for the Glasgow and Clyde Valley*, East Dumbartonshire Council, East Renfrewshire Council, Glasgow City Council, Inverclyde Council, North Lanarkshire Council, Renfrewshire Council, South Lanarkshire Council, West Dumbartonshire Council.

Meller, H. (1981) Patrick Geddes 1854–1932, in Cherry, G.E. (ed.) *Pioneers in British Planning*, The Architectural Press, London.

Index